MW00844732

Depression and Other Mental Health Issues

Aurora Tompar-Tiu, M.D.
Juliana Sustento-Seneriches, M.D.

Depression and Other Mental Health Issues

The Filipino American Experience

Manufactured in the United States of America. Nearly all Jossey-Bass books and jackets are printed on recycled paper that contains at least 50 percent recycled waste, including 10 percent postconsumer waste. Many of our materials are also printed with vegetable-based inks; during the printing process these inks emit fewer volatile organic compounds (VOCs) than petroleum-based inks. VOCs contribute to the formation of smog.

Library of Congress Cataloging-in-Publication Data

Tiu, Aurora Tompar-, date.
Depression and other mental health issues : the Filipino American experience / Aurora Tompar-Tiu, Juliana Sustento-Seneriches. —1st ed.
p. cm. — (A joint publication in the Jossey-Bass social and behavioral science series and the Jossey-Bass health series)
Includes bibliographical references and index.
ISBN 0-7879-0041-9 (hb)
1. Filipino Americans—Mental health. 2. Depression, Mental—United States. 3. Psychiatry, Transcultural—United States. 4. Filipino Americans—Mental health services. I. Seneriches, Juliana Sustento-, date. II. Title. III. Series: Jossey-Bass social and behavioral science series. IV. Series: Jossey-Bass health series.
[DNLM: 1. Depressive Disorder—ethnology—San Francisco. 2. Mental Disorders—ethnology—San Francisco. 3. Asian Americans—psychology. 4. Cultural Characteristics. WM 171 T623d 1994]
RC451.5.F54T56 1994
616.89'0089'9921073—dc20
DNLM/DLC
for Library of Congress 94-27879
CIP

FIRST EDITION
HB Printing 10 9 8 7 6 5 4 3 2 1 *Code 94125*

A joint publication in
The Jossey-Bass
Social and Behavioral Science Series
and
The Jossey-Bass Health Series

Contents

Tables, Figures, and Exhibit

Chapter 1

Chapter 2

Chapter 3

Chapter 4

To my husband, Dr. Victoriano Q. Tiu, who gave me the encouragement and understanding I needed to make this book a reality; to our children, Gladys, Carl, Simon Peter, and Marie Alys; and to my parents, Francisco and Leonora Tompar.

–A. T. T.

To my husband, Candido F. Seneriches, Jr., and our daughters, Liana and Candice, for their support and patience throughout this project; to my parents, Dominador and Lolita Sustento; and to my aunt, Patria S. Jean, all of whom encouraged my interest in medicine and writing.

–J. S. S.

Preface

The United States continues to attract masses of immigrants to its shores. These immigrants carry with them their own distinct cultures and unique ways of dealing with the inherently discordant process of immigration.

Since 1960, the Republic of the Philippines has been second only to Mexico as the country of origin of most immigrants (Fawcett, Arnold, and Minocha, 1984). Between 1970 and 1980, the Filipino American population increased by 113 percent and in every year since 1960 more than 43,000 Filipinos have come to the United States. The 1990 census officially accounted for 1.4 million Filipino Americans. Most are first-generation immigrants, and 45 percent settle in California. In the next ten years, Filipinos are likely to surpass Chinese immigrants to become the largest Asian immigrant group, at an estimated size of over 2 million (Bouvier and Agresta, 1987). By that time, one out of every four Asian Americans will be a Filipino American.

Yet, in spite of this significant population growth, little is known about the mental health needs and concerns of Filipino Americans. Much less is known about how effectively (if at all) they utilize the mental health system and treatment approaches in their host country.

Filipino Depression Research Project

The Filipino Depression Research Project, discussed in this book, is an attempt to study the prevalence and manifestations of clinical depression among Filipino Americans and the psycho-sociocultural profile of this ethnic group. Clinical depression is considered the most common mental health problem among immigrants, and since the majority of Filipino Americans are first-generation immigrants, it can be predicted that many of them are at risk for depression. The unavailability of familiar social support, unmet expectations, unemployment and underemployment, changes in social status, legal and immigration problems, overcrowding and housing problems, the challenge of mastering a new culture and language, and physical illnesses are common stressors that drain the mental, emotional, and physical resources of immigrants. Moreover, the economic impact of depression is also severe, in terms of loss of productivity, poor physical health, increased morbidity and mortality, absenteeism, and disruption of family life and child rearing. In terms of human suffering, the cost of depression is immeasurable; the long-term risk of suicide in clinical depression is about 15 percent (Teuting, Koslow, and Hirschfeld, 1981).

The research project discussed in this book afforded a look into the cross-cultural aspects of mental health and mental health care in this particular immigrant group. It provided a stimulus for the integration of emerging observations and past studies related to the mental health of this group, for the sharing of clinical experiences involving Filipino American clients, and for the laying of the groundwork whose result is this book. For example, the depression study showed that the rate of depression in the Filipino American community is 27.3 percent (Tompar-Tiu, 1990). Out of the 38,265 Filipinos in the San Francisco Bay Area (1980 census data), 10,000 to 14,000 would be expected to be depressed enough to need some form of mental health care. Yet Tolentino (1990) notes that out of 305 depressed clients seen from January 1987 to April 1988 at the South of Market Mental Health Clinic, in an area heavily populated with Filipinos, only 21 were

Filipinos, and only 11 of these patients were diagnosed as having major depression, dysthymia, or an adjustment disorder with depressive features. This indicates that clinically depressed Filipino Americans in the San Francisco Bay Area were not getting care at their local mental health clinic.

This finding opens up a whole array of questions about Filipino Americans' understanding of clinical depression, about how they deal with this disorder (if at all), and about how they see their host country's mental health care system and its available treatments. Are other mental disorders similarly dealt with by patients and families in this immigrant group? This question heightens awareness of community issues that may have some bearing on the group's mental health. What aspects of the native country's geography and history, Filipino immigration patterns, traditional Filipino family systems and beliefs, and the Philippine mental health care system may have formed current attitudes toward mental illness and treatments in the host country? How can effective preventive measures be planned? How can treatments be made more accessible and effective?

Through the window that is the Filipino Depression Research Project, a comprehensive and ever-expanding cross-cultural perspective comes into view. We hope that a cross-cultural understanding of the Filipino American experience in mental health—although it may raise still more provocative questions and reveal the need for further studies—will serve as a prototype for understanding other immigrant groups as well.

Audience

Depression and Other Mental Health Issues is intended for clinicians, researchers, teachers, and students in psychiatry, psychology, social work, anthropology, and other related fields. It attempts to provide both historical and cultural frameworks for addressing the mental health problems of Filipino Americans. It also presents guidelines on providing culturally sensitive mental health services for this group. We do not know of any other work that addresses all the issues presented here.

Overview of the Contents

Chapter One briefly describes Philippine geography, languages, and history, as well as Filipino Americans' immigration history, patterns and problems, and demographic and socioeconomic profiles in relation to other Asian ethnic groups.

In Chapter Two, we describe the Filipino depression study, its methodology, and its findings on the prevalence, manifestations, and severity of clinical depression in the group studied. Vignettes illustrate cognitive, motivational, and physical symptoms, as well as the severity of clinical depression. Medical causes of depression, such as hypothyroidism and other endocrine disorders, as well as medications are also discussed.

Chapter Three focuses on psychosociocultural profiles of clinically depressed and nondepressed Filipino American participants. The findings encompass sociodemographic data, immigration-related issues, family and work history, expectations and goals, stressors, beliefs and concepts, coping resources and responses, personality traits, and history of separation from the primary caregiver. Knowledge of these psychosociocultural profiles will help clinicians and mental health providers understand their clients and provide culturally sensitive interventions.

Chapter Four emphasizes significant sociocultural influences on manifestation of particular mental disorders, such as schizophrenia, acute psychoses, panic disorder, adjustment disorder, and culture-bound syndromes. Clinical observations and studies of the sociocultural influences and immigration processes that affect the presentation of these mental disorders are also discussed. Case studies illustrate the various disorders.

Chapter Five provides an overview of special issues concerning the mental health of Filipino American children, adolescents, and seniors. It also discusses AIDS, drug abuse, marital problems, and immigration problems. The chapter offers some cross-cultural perspectives on forensic psychiatry, with emphasis on language and communication, child-rearing practices, and legal issues in the workplace. Vignettes highlight some of the issues that need to be considered in cross-cultural forensic psychiatry.

Chapter Six describes the Filipino family, its structure

and its dynamics, as well as the characteristics of Filipino men and women and their traditional values. It also highlights some significant sociocultural factors affecting the mental health of Filipino Americans.

Chapter Seven presents an overview of the Philippine mental health system, as described by Filipino immigrants, in comparison with the U.S. system. Traditional attitudes toward illness, beliefs about causes, and factors that affect the process of acculturation are also discussed in this chapter.

Chapter Eight provides practical guidelines for cross-cultural assessment of Filipino American clients, stressing the need for more studies in this area. We also highlight cultural traits and values affecting communication.

Chapter Nine presents various techniques, interventions, and issues in the treatment of mental disorders among Filipino Americans, with the treatment of clinical depression as a prototype. Vignettes illustrate some of the problems in the treatment of mental health disorders. Practical counseling and cognitive therapy are among the interventions discussed.

We hope that *Depression and Other Mental Health Issues* will stimulate more research and more publications on Filipino Americans and that it will inspire students and mental health professionals to learn more about cross-cultural psychiatry.

Acknowledgments

Our heartfelt thanks and appreciation go to the board members and staff of the St. Francis Foundation and St. Francis Memorial Hospital, particularly Donald Doyle, who believed in the goals of the research project and in the importance of providing adequate mental health services to minorities.

We especially want to thank Dr. Douglas Anderson, former director of the Western Psychiatric Center of St. Francis Hospital and co-investigator of the Filipino Depression Research Project. He provided guidance and clinical and administrative support, as well as insightful recommendations in implementing the project and writing this book. Dr. Edgardo B. Tolentino, co-investigator of the Filipino Depression Research Project and coauthor of Chapter Nine, shared his excellent clinical experiences and skills.

We also appreciate the clerical and editorial support of Candy Bandong, Irene Chikiamco, Rose Marie P. Constantino, Marian Esver, and Cecilia Flannery, as well as Arceli Dew Jamandre's organizational skills and support at crucial times.

The insightful suggestions of Dr. Ver Enriquez, Teresita Quisumbing, Gaspar Sandalla, and Dr. Steve Wager were very useful in updating this book's references and data. Dr. Luisito Claudio's assistance in editing the text and his translations from English to Tagalog and Leonora Gonzalez's translations of questionnaires are also appreciated.

The following people provided us with materials and shared their experiences and knowledge: Dr. Ching Piao Chien, Dr. Eyong Kim, Dr. Luke Kim, Dr. Lourdes Ladrido-Ignacio, Dr. Hsi Hyung Lee, Melan McBride, Ricardo Muñoz, Dr. Joe Yamamoto, and Han Yun.

We would also like to thank Susan Lutes, Bruce Hasenkamp, Richard Slottow, and John Williams for their enduring support during the research and writing of this book.

For research and clerical work, we thank Dr. Patrick Calalang, Napoleon Fusilero, Michael Husmillo, and Maria Luisa Sustento.

Alice Pierotti, our Filipino American patients, and our research participants inspired us to write this book. Our families, especially our husbands and children, gave us the loving support to finish our task.

Finally, we wish to thank all the Filipino Americans who participated in the research.

October 1994

Aurora Tompar-Tiu, M.D.
Teaneck, New Jersey

Juliana Sustento-Seneriches, M.D.
Pleasanton, California

The Authors

AURORA TOMPAR-TIU, M.D., was the principal investigator of the five-year Filipino Depression Research Project, conducted at St. Francis Memorial Hospital in collaboration with San Francisco General Hospital. She has also served as chair of the research committee of the Filipino Mental Health Resource Group in San Francisco. She received her B.S. degree in science (1968) from the University of San Carlos and her M.D. degree (1972) from the Cebu Institute of Medicine, Philippines. She had postgraduate training in family and community medicine and later pursued Ph.D. studies in psychology at the University of the Philippines.

Currently, she is a fellow in child and adolescent psychiatry at St. Luke's/Roosevelt Hospital Center, Columbia University College of Physicians and Surgeons, New York, where she continues to explore her interest in cross-cultural psychiatry. In collaboration with various Philippine service and research agencies, she has conducted community- and hospital-based studies on the mental development of Filipino children and the effects of environmental stimulation on their development. She has also worked with UNICEF as a technical consultant for a community-based research project on childhood disabilities.

She arrived in the United States in 1984, as a visiting scholar at St. Francis Memorial Hospital, and received a research grant from the St. Francis Foundation to study clinical depression among Filipino Americans.

JULIANA SUSTENTO-SENERICHES, M.D., maintains a full-time private psychiatric practice in Pleasanton, California, and serves as councilor of the Northern California Psychiatric Association. She was president of the East Bay Psychiatric Association and a founding fellow of the Pacific Rim College of Psychiatrists. She received her M.D. degree (1966) from the University of the Philippines and became a psychiatric resident and teaching fellow (1967) at Harvard Medical School–Boston City Hospital Department of Psychiatry. In 1968, she became chief resident of the hospital's Psychiatric Outpatient Department. A post-residency fellowship in Boston State Hospital's community psychiatry program helped inspire her abiding interest in cross-cultural psychiatry. After years of work in community psychiatry and private practice on the East Coast, she returned to the Philippines to practice and teach. She moved her practice to California in 1984.

She has written numerous scientific papers, a book, and book chapters, mostly on the Filipino psychiatric patient.

Depression and Other Mental Health Issues

Chapter 1

Understanding the Filipino American Experience

To understand Filipino Americans and their mental health concerns, clinicians must be knowledgeable about Philippine geography, history, and immigration patterns. In this book, the term *Filipino Americans* refers to Filipinos in the United States, regardless of place of birth and immigration status. They include immigrants, permanent residents, United States–born citizens, students, businesspeople, temporary workers, and tourists who decide to stay permanently in the United States.

Geography

The Philippines is a tropical archipelago composed of about 7,107 islands in southeast Asia. Its neighbors include Taiwan to the north and Malaysia and Indonesia to the south. The archipelago is divided into three island groups: Luzon (in the north), Visayas (in the central area), and Mindanao (in the south). It has a land area slightly larger than Nevada's (Agoncillo and Guerrero, 1987) and an estimated 1990 population of 64 million, with 40 percent residing in urban communities, particularly Metro-Manila, Cebu, and Davao, the largest cities. Sixty percent live in rural agricultural areas throughout the islands. The archipelago lies slightly above the equator and is bounded on the east by the Pacific Ocean, on the west by the China Sea, and on the south by the Celebes Sea. It has two seasons: rainy or wet (June to October), and dry (November to May).

The Archipelago Effect

We theorize that the archipelago setting of the Philippines helps significantly in creating the pockets of strong regionalism consistently observed in the Philippine setting, with regional customs carried on by first-generation Filipino Americans. Poor transportation facilities and a poor economy reinforce the relative isolation of the different island and regional groups and foster the need for extended families, the emergence of dominant clans, the use of more than one hundred different languages, and many native cultural values. The stigma of mental illness, even within the family, is more visible and more strongly felt in an island setting. The use of *hiya,* or shame, to curtail unwanted social behavior becomes more potent in a place where individual identities are linked to families visible to or known by one another. Traveling from one island or region to another for advanced education and livelihood will also be common in such a setting, and so the precedent is set for immigration to other countries, often for the advancement of the family to which the immigrant continues to be linked.

Languages

About seventy-five ethnolinguistic groups, speaking more than one hundred different languages, comprise the Filipino population (Lamzon, 1978). Pilipino (Tagalog) is the national language. English is the second official language. Some residents also speak Spanish. The eight major ethnic groups, each with its distinct language, are the Tagalog (29.6 percent), the Cebuano (24.2 percent), the Ilocano (10.3 percent), the Ilonggo (9.2 percent), the Bikolano (5.5 percent), the Waray (4 percent), the Kapampangan (2.8 percent), and the Pangasinenses (less than

1 percent). Each group is perceived as having some stereotypical characteristics. For example, the Ilocanos are seen as thrifty and hardworking, the Ilonggos as gentle, the Warays as tough and fierce, and the Cebuanos as warm and spontaneous. Language and ethnicity divides the Filipinos and may also explain the regionalism that Filipinos bring with them when they immigrate. It is important to recognize differences among the Filipinos, but it is also vital to know that, in spite of their regionalism, they have the tendency to perceive themselves more as one people when they become immigrants (Anderson, 1983).

History

Knowledge of the historical background of Filipino Americans gives mental health professionals a better understanding of the mental health problems and issues facing Filipino Americans.

Precolonization

Historical records show that before the Spaniards arrived, the Filipinos had their own culture, with their own customs, arts, literature, religious beliefs, laws, judicial processes, government, and social structures. Their culture was molded in response to their environment and was influenced by their neighbors—the Malays, the Chinese (many of whom migrated to the Philippines), the Indonesians, and the Asian Indians. Presumed to have emerged from the same base culture, the Filipinos, the Malays, and the Indonesians are "coequal as ethnic groups, without anyone being the dominant group, racially or culturally" (Jocano, 1975). Relations with China also enriched the Filipino culture, as reflected in the adoption of Chinese words, Chinese methods of cooking, mining, and manufacturing, and the use of such items as umbrellas, slippers, and gongs. Chinese traders are said to have noted the honesty of ancient Filipinos in business dealings.

Asian Indian influences are evident in the Tagalog language (which has words similar to words found in Sanskrit) and in modes of dress and architectural art.

The Arabs introduced Islam in the southern part of the Philippines in about 1380. The Filipino Muslims, mostly in Mindanao and Sulu, refused Catholic conversion by the Spaniards and maintain their culture and traditions today.

Agricultural society was divided into three classes: nobles, freemen (*maharlika*), and dependents (*alipin*) (Agoncillo and Guerrero, 1987). Unlike slaves, the dependents, particularly the *aliping namamahay,* lived with their families in their own homes but helped their masters on their farms, built their masters' homes and served their masters' guests. The *aliping sagigilid,* another group of dependents, had no property and could marry only with their masters' consent. (A modern counterpart of the *alipin* is still found in many middle- and upper-income Filipino families who have household helpers (*katulong*) and *yayas,* people mainly responsible for child care. Housekeepers and *yayas* usually live with the master's family and may be treated like members of the family. Unlike the *aliping sagigilid,* they are allowed to own property and can marry without the consent of their masters or employees. Because of recent immigration to other countries, however, there is now a dearth of these helpers in the big cities.)

The precolonial unit of government was the *barangay,* headed by the *datu,* or chieftain, and composed of thirty to one hundred families. The *babaylans* were the keepers of the sacred traditions and are considered to have been the first Filipino psychologists. The *bagani* were the protectors of the territory. Indigenous customary laws and orders punished such crimes as rape, incest, murder, trespassing, larceny, the abuse and disrespect of elders, women, and children, and the destruction or killing of trees and animals (such as crocodiles and sharks). The indigenous Philippine religion taught respect for ancestors, for nature, and for one's fellows. *Bathala* was considered to be the creator of humans and of the earth; environmental spirits (*anitos*), the various gods (of love, death, or the harvest), and soul spirits were presumed to be immortal. The ancient Filipinos also worshipped animals (for example, crocodiles and birds), sacred trees, the sun, and the moon (Agoncillo and Guerrero, 1987).

Colonization

After its discovery in 1521 by Ferdinand Magellan, who named the archipelago after King Philip II of Spain, the Philippines was a colony of Spain for more than three centuries. The Catholic Church was the main Spanish contribution of colonization: the Philippines is the only predominantly Catholic country in Asia. At present, 83 percent of Filipinos are Roman Catholics, 9 percent are Protestants, and 5 percent are Muslims. There are two independent Filipino churches: Iglesia ni Christo (the Church of Christ) and Aglipay (the Philippine Independent Church). Spanish priests played a significant role in colonizing the Filipinos and grouped the *barangays* into religious communities. By converting the natives to Catholicism, the priests used the notion of God as a strong ally in their colonial tactics, exploiting the natives and promoting a colonial mentality of ignorance, fanaticism, passivity, and resignation. Fear of divine retribution was added to fear of corporal punishment, which made it easier for one priest to rule a whole community, since rebellion against the priest meant rebellion against God. The Spaniards were not able to conquer the Filipino Muslims through religion, but they did promote alienation between Muslims and Christians, which still exists.

Forced labor, unjust taxation, and political suppression resulted in the Filipinos' revolt against the Spaniards. From the very beginning, the natives had resisted the conquerors. Magellan was killed by a native, Lapu-Lapu, in Mactan, Cebu. There were several small, scattered revolts against the Spaniards, but it was not until 1896 that a national Filipino revolution, led by Andres Bonifacio, ended Spanish rule. The result was the establishment of the first Philippine Republic, on June 12, 1896, headed by Emilio Aguinaldo. In 1898, after the Spanish-American War, Spain ceded the Philippines to the United States for $20 million.

For forty-eight years (1898–1946) the Philippines was a U.S. protectorate. The most significant United States influence was the establishment of a system of public education throughout the country (although the Spaniards had established the first Filipino university, the University of Santo Tomas, in 1611). Under the Spanish regime, only the upper class had enjoyed access to higher learning, but the U.S.-established educational system was open to all Filipinos regardless of social class. Today, the Philippines has one of the highest literacy rates (88 percent) in Asia, and men and women have equal opportunity for higher education (Andres, 1987).

Mass education, established by the Americans, initially used American books and teachers and began the "Americanization" of the Filipinos. Continuous exposure to American mass media and products reinforced the "stateside mentality" of many Filipinos (Andres, 1987). The English language, public education, and improved health, sewage, and road systems were other significant American contributions. The Filipinos embraced the American culture and language and imitated the Western way of life at the expense of their own cultural and national identities. They became great consumers of American goods. They thought that the United States was the land of freedom, of "milk and honey." This idea fostered the "Filipino dream"—emigration to the United States, in search of better opportunities.

Postcolonization

Even after the Philippines gained independence from the United States in 1946, the Filipinos continued to pattern their educational system and form of government after those of the American colonizers. The use of the English language, as well as the presence of American books, literature, and movies, encouraged the "de-Filipinization of Filipinos" (Agoncillo and Guerrero, 1987) and helped foster a colonial attitude and way of thinking. American culture and goods were considered superior to those of the Philippines. The American style of living was imitated, which resulted in the diminution of Filipino nationalism and traditional Filipino values. Materialism became an important aspect of the Filipino consciousness. Although religion was still central to Filipino life, the drive for financial success and social status became fertile ground for graft and corruption.

Many Filipino intellectuals and students resisted American influences in the political, social, and economic aspects of Filipino life. The Philippine government implemented measures intended to enhance Filipino nationalism (for example, using Filipino languages in the primary and elementary schools).

Nevertheless, socioeconomic and political problems under the Marcos dictatorship forced Filipinos to look for better opportunities outside their native land. Many left for the United States, other industrial countries, and the Middle East (particularly Saudi Arabia). The political and socioeconomic problems reached their peak toward the end of the Marcos years. About 75 percent of Filipinos were living below the poverty line, earning the equivalent of approximately $1,000 a year for a family of six. In 1986, a successful, peaceful, bloodless revolution, with the cooperation of the Catholic Church, forced the end of the Marcos regime.

Having survived four centuries of colonialism, with its legacies of colonial mentality, fatalism, subservience, and division, and having broken free of a twenty-year period of official governmental corruption and injustice, Filipinos at home turned to the future with new hope. They still face many hurdles and a persistent divisiveness.

Immigration History and Patterns

Filipinos were the earliest Asian immigrants to the United States. They settled in Louisiana in 1763. They came—before the Chinese, and before the arrival of the *Mayflower*—as crewmen on the Philippine-made galleon *San Pablo,* which travelled from Cebu, the oldest city in the Philippines, to Mexico during the period of the Spanish-Mexican galleon trade (1565–1815). Forced labor and maltreatment at the hands of their Spanish colonizers prompted the Filipinos to jump ship in Acapulco, where they introduced the process of making wine (*tuba*) from coconuts. Later, these Filipinos took refuge in southeastern Louisiana. Known as *Manilamen,* these seafaring Filipinos and their descendants, the Filipino cajuns, contributed to the rich culture of Louisiana, where they initiated the process of sun-drying shrimp for export. Since the arrival of the first Manilamen, there have been four periods of Filipino immigration to the United States: 1763–1906, 1906–1934, 1945–1965, and 1965 and thereafter.

First Period (1763–1906)

This period saw the arrival of the Manilamen in Louisiana. There followed domestic helpers, steamship crew members, stowaways, mariners, and others who wanted adventure and a better life in America. In 1870, the Sociedad de Beneficencia de los Hispano Filipinos de Nueva Orleans, the first benevolent club organized by Filipinos in the United States, was established. Most of the members were men who spoke their native languages as well as Spanish. Some went on to California. A Filipino was probably one of the founders of the Pueblo de Nuestra Señora Reina de los Angeles (Los Angeles City), in 1781. Others went to Hawaii, Washington, and Alaska, where they worked on whaling ships with the Eskimos.

Second Period (1906–1934)

This wave comprised mostly young (fourteen–twenty-nine years), single, uneducated or poorly educated men from the rural areas of the Ilocos and Visayas regions. The first fifteen Filipinos arrived in Hawaii on board the *Doric* in December 1906. They were recruited for work on the sugarcane plantations and proudly called themselves *sakadas,* or contract laborers. From 1907 to 1919, the Hawaiian Sugar Planters' Association experimented with the *sakadas* to replace the Japanese, after Japan restricted the migration of Japanese laborers. The experiment was successful, and more Filipinos were recruited. The influx of Filipino laborers greatly increased after 1924, when the Japanese were excluded by the new immigration act (Melendy, 1974). The Filipino laborers in the railroads and the mines were like the Chinese immigrants, who had come without their wives and families. They were considered not to have any intention of becoming an integral part of the United States society, and to have high hopes of returning to their homeland. Many of them remain single today and are referred to as *manongs* (older brothers). They are also called *old-timers* by more recent immigrants.

In addition to the plantation workers, a small group of Filipino scholars, the *pensionados,* were sent to the United States by the Philippine territorial government, which subsidized their education. After completing their studies, they went back to the Philippines to take responsible positions in government or the universities. Later Filipino immigrants came to the United States to work, study, or seek opportunities to improve their economic condition and join their families. Calling themselves *pinoys,* they worked on California farms and in the Alaskan canneries (Vallangca, 1977). They provided cheap farm labor and were considered stoop-laborers, but they contributed tremendously to economic growth wherever they worked. Manual and menial jobs that most white persons did not want were given to the Filipinos. Apart from being farm laborers and cannery workers, they were domestic helpers in hotels, hospitals, and homes, and they worked as busboys and janitors. They were also discriminated against in many places, such as restaurants and residential areas. They were called *brown monkeys,* and many white American men viewed them as an economic and social threat, competing for jobs and women.

Because the Philippines was a territory of the United States, Filipino immigrants to the United States were considered U.S. nationals but were not allowed to vote, own property, start businesses, or marry members of the Caucasian race. There was a sex imbalance, and the ratio of Filipino men to women in the United States was 20:1 in 1920 and 14:1 in 1930 (Lasker, 1974). Those men who were married had left their wives and children in the Philippines. Many other Filipino men married late in life, and still others went back to the Philippines to marry or to visit their families. In 1934, as a result of the Tydings-McDuffie Act, the Philippines was changed from a United States territory to a commonwealth, and Filipinos became aliens instead of nationals. The act also limited the annual quota of Filipino immigrants to fifty.

The *pinoys* were concentrated mostly in rural areas—the San Joaquin Valley, Sacramento, and Salinas in California—

but also in some urban places, such as San Francisco, Los Angeles, New York, and Chicago. Chinese and Japanese immigrants had their Chinatowns and Japantowns, and the so-called Manilatowns were like ghettos for *pinoys,* who frequently spent time in gambling places and dance halls after work. In spite of being underpaid, the Filipinos managed to send part of their hard-earned money to their relatives in the Philippines. They continued to work, proud that they were doing their best. Hoping that their dreams of a better life would come true, they suffered social discrimination, as the other minorities also did, as well as the negative psychological and emotional effects of realizing that the land of freedom and equality that they had envisioned was not after all living up to their hopes and expectations.

The Filipino immigrants' strength of character and sense of humor helped them cope with adversity, however. They organized themselves into labor unions and engaged in collective bargaining with their employers. They formed church and subethnic social organizations that provided mutual aid and support, although these organizations were not as strong and organized as the Chinese *hui kuan* (an association whose members spoke the same dialect, or who came from the same district or ethnic group in China) or the Chinese Benevolent Association that governed Chinatown. Most of the *pinoys* (like the *sakadas*) were considered unskilled laborers throughout their lives, but some did manage to study and enhance their livelihood, and so did their children.

The majority of *pinoys,* who remained single, continued to be relegated to the same low social status, unable to obtain more education or higher-paying jobs. According to Urban Associates (1974), 63 percent of poor elderly Filipinos are males who still live by themselves. These *manongs* have managed to comfort themselves with the camaraderie of fellow Filipinos in their locales.

Third Period (1945–1965)

The immigrants during this period consisted of war veterans, military personnel and their families, students, and professionals with their wives and children. This wave comprised more women and families than the second wave. The "brown monkeys" were now called *little brown brothers*. They had fought with the Americans during World War II (Vallangca, 1977). The professionals (doctors, nurses, engineers, technicians, and accountants) were mostly from urban areas and middle-income families. The "brain drain" began in this period, when poor countries were losing many of their best-educated people to rich countries.

Wherever Filipinos resided, such as on the West Coast, the immigrants contributed significantly to the economy, to religious, community, political, and labor organizations, to science and art, and to music and entertainment. They were faithful to most of the American institutions where they worked, in spite of the economic exploitation and racism they experienced.

Fourth Period (1965 and Thereafter)

The abolition, in 1965, of the quota system instituted by the Tydings-McDuffie Act attracted the largest influx of immigrants in history to the United States, mostly Asians and Hispanics. Filipinos continued to arrive in the thousands and became one of the fastest-growing ethnic minorities in many states, although still predominantly in such western states as California, Hawaii, Washington, and Oregon. Professionals from the medical and nursing fields, dentists, engineers, teachers, and students comprised the majority of the new arrivals. By contrast with the first and second waves, people in this wave were highly educated, spoke English, and came from middle-income families in urban areas. Predominantly female (wives and children, mail-order brides, working women, and students), these immigrants came mainly because of the socioeconomic and political problems in the Philippines and because of their own wishes to join spouses and families (the Family Reunification Program of the Immigration Reform Act of 1965 had made it possible for family members to be reunited in the United States).

In 1972, shortly after the declaration of martial law in the Philippines by President Marcos, the latest part of this wave began to arrive on tourist, business, student, and fiancee visas.

Many tourists (mostly professionals and businesspeople), not wanting to return, tried to find employers who would hire them as temporary workers and sponsor them in the United States. Some gained permanent-resident status by marrying U.S. citizens (some even paid their prospective spouses). Tourists, students, and businesspeople who stayed after their visas had expired were called *TNT* (*tago ng tago,* hiding and hiding) by the Filipino community. Some were also called *NPAs* (no permanent address) or *CIA* (California illegal aliens). They continued to hide from immigration officers, managing to work illegally, but were frequently exploited by their employers.

The Filipino American Population

The 1990 U.S. Census accounts for 1,406,770 Filipino Americans, the second-largest population of Asian Americans in the United States, after Chinese Americans. They will continue to be one of the fastest-growing Asian groups. It is estimated that by the year 2000, the Filipino American population will reach 2.1 million, or 21 percent of all Asian Americans (Bouvier and Agresta, 1987), more than any other Asian group in the United States (see Figure 1.1). Immigration is the major reason for this projected rapid rate of increase. With the revised Immigration and Naturalization Act, yearly immigration increased, from 2,545 in 1965 to 31,203 in 1970. This increase made the Philippines the second greatest "exporter" (after Mexico) of immigrants to the United States. Since 1980, more than 43,000 Filipino immigrants have arrived in the United States every year. Between 1970 and 1980, the Filipino American population increased by 113 percent, to 781,894.

In 1980, 45.8 percent of all Filipino Americans lived in California, comprising a population of 358,378, or 1.5 percent of the state's population. They were the state's largest Asian American minority (Bouvier and Martin, 1985) and continued to lead among Asian Americans in California in the 1990 U.S. Census (see Figure 1.2). In 1970, 37 percent of all new immigrants to San Francisco were Filipinos. In 1987, 58,300 Filipinos emigrated to the United States, and 50,697 emigrated in 1988. In spite of this tremendous population growth, there is still very

Figure 1.1. Asian American Population in the United States.

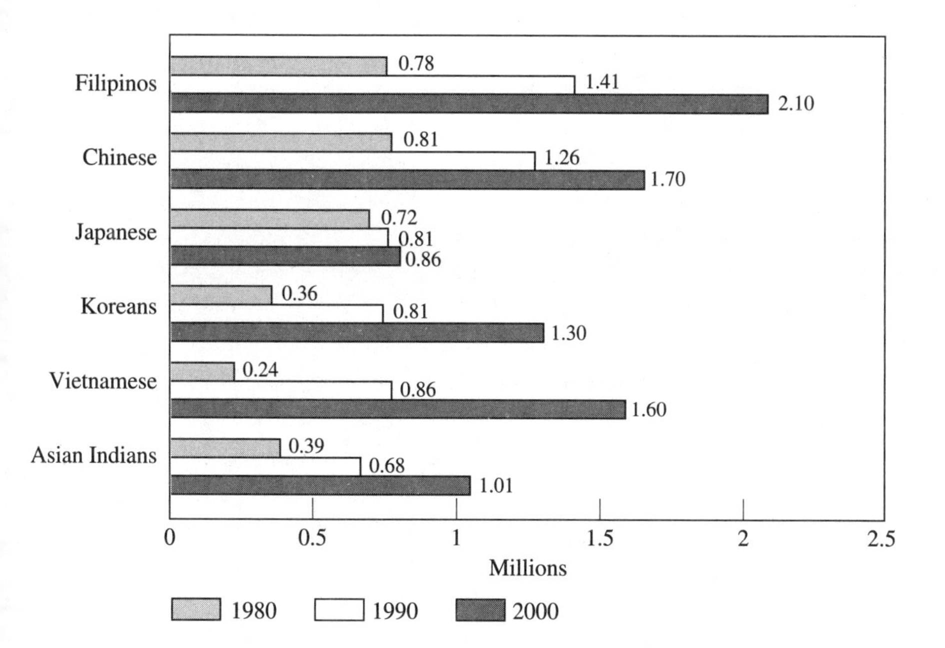

Sources: Adapted from Bouvier and Agresta, 1987; Gardner, Robey, and Smith, 1989.

little published information concerning Filipino Americans and their mental health status (Hart, 1979; Anderson, 1983).

By comparison with other Asian American groups, Filipino Americans still have a lower median annual income per full-time worker ($13,690) than do Chinese, Japanese, Asian Indian, Korean, and white Americans but a higher median income than Vietnamese, Hispanic, and African Americans (U.S. Bureau of the Census, 1991). Although the majority of Filipino Americans are educated, many are still underemployed and underpaid. Among Asian American women, Filipino women have the highest participation rate in the work force (Gardner, Robey, and Smith, 1989). Most of the new arrivals since 1970 are predominantly females in the productive age group. Additional socioeconomic characteristics of Filipino Americans and other Asians are shown in Table 1.1.

Figure 1.2. Asian American Population in California.

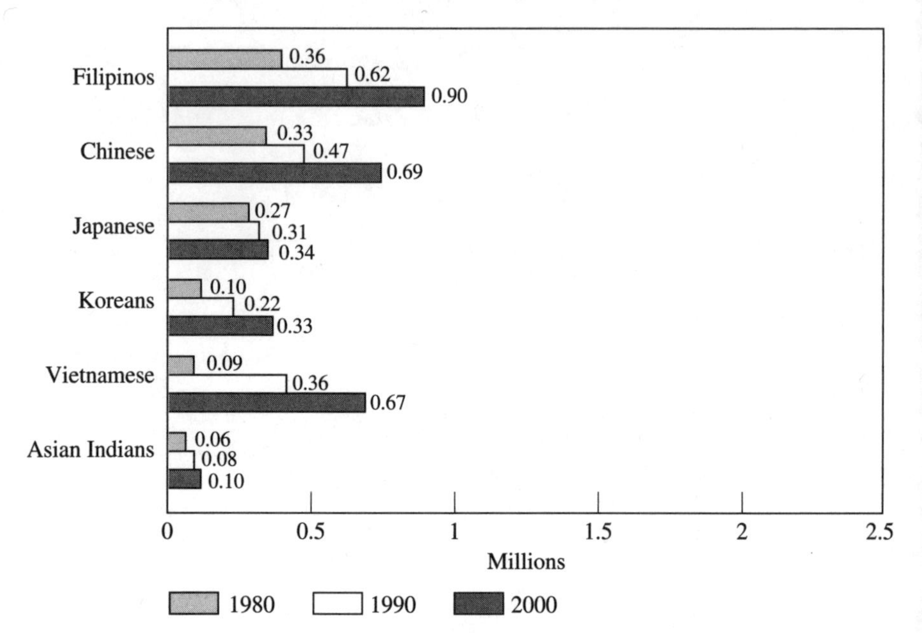

Source: Adapted from Bouvier and Martin, 1985.

Conclusion

Although Filipino Americans are the second largest Asian group in the United States, there is still a lack of information regarding them and their mental health profile. This chapter's overview of the geographical and historical background of Filipino Americans—as well as their immigration patterns and demographic characteristics—should help facilitate a better understanding of this ethnic group and hopefully increase sensitivity to their mental health needs and issues.

With the influx of immigrants to the United States from around the world, the Filipino American experience may serve as a prototype for understanding other ethnic groups and should stimulate more research on immigrants' common mental health problems.

Table 1.1. Demographic and Socioeconomic Characteristics of Filipinos and Other Asian Americans.

	Filipinos	*Chinese*	*Japanese*	*Indian*	*Korean*	*Vietnamese*
Population (1990)	1,406,770	1,645,472	847,562	815,447	798,849	614,547
Population (thousands, 1980)	782	812	716	387	357	245
Immigrants admitted to U.S. (thousands, 1988)	50.7	28.7	4.5	26.3	34.7	25.8
Median income per full-time worker (in 1979 dollars)	13,690	15,753	16,829	18,707	14,224	11,641
Percentage of women (16 and over) in labor force as family householders	79.0	70.3	72.5	58.2	71.1	56.0
Percentage of households with income from public assistance	10.0	6.6	4.2	4.5	6.2	28.1
Percentage of families below poverty level	6.2	10.5	4.2	7.4	13.1	35.1
Average family size	4.2	3.7	3.6	3.5	4.9	5.2
Median income (in 1979 dollars)	23,687	22,559	27,354	24,993	20,459	12,840
Percentage of unemployed in the civilian labor force	4.8	3.6	3.0	5.8	5.7	8.2
Percentage with fewer than five years of school	7.0	10.3	2.3	3.1	4.0	10.3
Percentage with four years of high school or more education	74.2	71.3	81.6	80.1	75.1	62.2
Percentage with four or more years of college	37.0	36.6	26.4	51.9	33.7	12.9

Sources: U.S. Bureau of the Census, 1991; Gardner, Robey, and Smith, 1989.

Chapter 2

The Depression Study

Clinical depression is a universal mental health problem that must be studied adequately, particularly in high-risk groups, such as among immigrants, minorities, and refugees (Kuo, 1984; Beiser, 1988). Among Asian Americans, Filipino Americans have been identified as one of the high-risk groups for mental disorders, together with Vietnamese Americans and Pacific Islander Americans (for example, Samoan-Americans), because their social indicators, such as socioeconomic and employment status, are lower than those of Chinese Americans and Japanese Americans (Sue and Morishima, 1982). While the effects of mental disorders like depression on the quality of human life, productivity, family life, and child rearing are difficult to determine, loss of human resources because of suicide or destructive behaviors secondary to depression drains society's greatest wealth. Indeed, depression is a very expensive mental health problem in terms of human loss and suffering (Muñoz, 1987). The United States spends approximately $16.5 billion every year on the treatment of depression. This total includes such indirect costs as absenteeism and loss of or decreased productivity (Frank, Kamlet, and Stoudemire, 1985).

A community-based study in Seattle by Kuo (1984) on the prevalence of depression among East Asian Americans (Japanese, Chinese, Korean, and Filipino Americans) found that Filipino Americans had the second-highest mean score (after Korean Americans) on the Center for Epidemiological Studies Depression (CES-D) Scale (Radloff, 1977). A CES-D score of 16 or more is considered to denote clinical depression. In Kuo's study, 19.1 percent of the Asian American samples had clinical depression, given their CES-D scores of 16 and above. The Filipino Americans also differed from the other groups on some second-factor CES-D items and on patterns of expressing depression. Kuo speculates (p. 452) that Spanish colonization (with Christian influences) and a correspondingly lesser influence of Confucian ethics in Philippine life may have a role in terms of whatever effects result from cultural heritage.

Several cross-cultural investigations of depression indicate that depression itself is not manifested uniformly across cultures (Marsella, 1980; Kleinman, 1982). In China, for example, the rate of depressive disorders is much lower than the rate of neurasthenic disorders; but, among the patients diagnosed as neurasthenic, 93 percent manifest the signs and symptoms of clinical depression (Kleinman, 1982). Therefore, there truly is a culturally based difference in the way depression is conceptualized and expressed. The prevalence of clinical depression among Filipinos "is very likely grossly underestimated" (Araneta, 1993, p. 391), mainly because of the cultural tendency of Filipinos to deny emotional problems (Lapuz, 1978), endure emotional suffering (Bulatao, 1963), and somatize emotional problems (Flaskerud and Soldevilla, 1986). Only those with psychotic depression are usually brought to mental health facilities; the mild and moderate forms of major depression are rarely identified and treated.

The Depression Study: Objectives and Methodology

In response to the increasing need for more studies on Filipino Americans' mental health, a study was conducted (Tompar-

Tiu, 1990) primarily to gather information on the depressive symptomatology and psychosocial profiles of clinically depressed versus nondepressed Filipino Americans. The study also attempted to find out how common depression is among Filipino Americans in community, outpatient, and inpatient settings.

The participants—Filipino Americans, native or foreign-born, but all residing in the United States—were recruited from inpatient and outpatient clinics and from Filipino communities in San Francisco and the rest of the San Francisco Bay area. Patients were recruited in person, with permission from their attending physicians, when they were admitted to hospitals or saw their doctors at the outpatient clinics. Participants from the Filipino communities were randomly selected from membership lists of Filipino organizations, social groups, and religious groups, and from lists of employees and students. Only one member per family was included, and relatives of participants were excluded. The participants were contacted by telephone or asked in person to participate in a study of the moods, health, and psychosocial profiles of Filipino Americans. Informed consent (with appropriate translation) was obtained from all participants in person.

Initially, the participants were interviewed with the demographic-profile section of a structured psychosocial questionnaire specifically developed and pretested for the study and translated into Tagalog for those who did not speak English. If the participant was eighteen or older and not in acute cardiopulmonary distress, not disoriented, and not suffering from obvious mental retardation, the interview lasted approximately ninety minutes. The mood-disorder portion of a structured clinical interview (Spitzer, Williams, and Gibbon, 1987) was used as a guide for identifying the presence of major or clinical depression and its severity. Participants found to have active suicidal ideation or suicide attempts were immediately referred for intervention or for possible admission to the psychiatric units of the participating hospitals. Before the first interview session ended, a symptom checklist (Derogatis, 1973), a depression inventory (Beck, 1961) and the CES-D scale were presented (in translation, as necessary) and explained to the participant. Participants received a demonstration on how to answer the questions. They were asked to fill the instruments out and return them during the second interview session (held within a week of the first session).

At the second ninety-minute session, the research physician interviewed the participant with a rating scale for depression (Hamilton, 1960), reviewed the filled-out instruments, and administered the remaining parts of the structured psychosocial questionnaire, which included an immigration profile, a family and work history, and questions about expectations and goals in life, stressors, coping resources and skills, concepts or beliefs about clinical depression, and childhood and adolescent history. Subsequent interview sessions were held at weekly intervals. By the second or third session, participants felt more comfortable talking about stressors and problems.

Participants who were referred or admitted to psychiatric units for major depression, with active suicidal ideation or attempts, were followed up within a week after referral, and more data were obtained from them. Participants with medical, legal, immigration, or psychosocial problems (such as unemployment or family problems) were referred to employment services, vocational programs, or psychosocial services in the community. A referral network was set up among Filipino mental health professionals and allied services, to provide immediate support and interventions for participants with identified psychosocial, medical, and psychiatric problems. Participants' attending physicians were given information (with the participants' permission) about significant findings.

Prevalence of Clinical Depression

In this study, conducted from 1986 to 1989, out of 400 Filipino American males and females eighteen and above who were asked to participate, 345 complied (a refusal rate of 13.8 percent). Table 2.1 shows the sample distribution according to recruitment setting (the community, medical or family health outpatient clinics, and medical or psychiatric inpatient units) and the prevalence of major depression or clinical depression according to severity and setting. Participants were considered to have clinical

Table 2.1. Prevalence of Clinical (Major) Depression Among Filipino Americans by Setting and Severity, 1986–1989.

Severity of Depression	*Community (n = 143)*		*Medical Outpatient (n = 100)*		*Medical Inpatient (n = 56)*		*Psychiatric Inpatient (n = 46)*	
Mild	14	9.8%	9	9%	6	10.7%	–	–
Moderate	15	10.5%	23	23%	9	16.1%	–	–
Severe	9	6.3%	18	18%	10	17.9%	4	8.7%
With psychotic features	1	0.6%	2	2%	1	1.8%	8	17.4%
Overall	39	27.3%	52	52%	26	46.4%	12	26.1%

Note: Severity is measured according to the criteria listed in the revised third edition of the *Diagnostic and Statistical Manual of Mental Disorders (DSM III-R)* (American Psychiatric Association, 1987).

depression if they met the diagnostic criteria for a major depressive episode (classified as mild, moderate, or severe, with or without psychotic features) of the *Diagnostic and Statistical Manual of Mental Disorders (DSM III-R)* (American Psychiatric Association, 1987).

A major depressive episode consists of at least five symptoms present for a minimum of two weeks that signify a change from former functioning with some impairment in occupational or social functions. The symptoms include dysphoric mood (depressed or irritable); loss of interest or lack of pleasure (one of these two symptoms must be present); sleep and appetite disturbances; changes in weight and energy levels; psychomotor retardation or agitation; problems with concentration, thinking, and attention; feelings of helplessness or worthlessness; excessive guilt and suicidal ideation/attempts; or frequent thoughts of death. These symptoms are not secondary to organic factors, a result of uncomplicated bereavement, or superimposed on other psychiatric disorders such as schizophrenia, delusional disorder, or psychotic disorders not otherwise specified.

Depression in the Community

As shown in Table 2.1, 27.3 percent of the community sample was found to have a major depressive episode or clinical depression of varying severity. This prevalence rate in the San Francisco Bay area Filipino community is higher than in the U.S. general adult population, where lifetime prevalence rates are usually reported as 10–20 percent (Muñoz, 1987). It is also higher than the combined lifetime rate of 26.7 percent for major and minor depression, as reported by Weissman and Myers (1978). Kuo (1984) predicts that any minority group that has experienced significant psychological and environmental stressors will have a higher rate of mental disorders than the rate found in the general population; the estimated higher prevalence found in this study supports Kuo's prediction, as well as the idea that rates of depression are increasing and are higher among individuals born about and after 1940 than among those born earlier.

Depression in Medical or Family Health Outpatient Clinics

Of all the recruitment settings, the outpatient clinics have the highest prevalence rate (52 percent) with severity rates of 9 percent mild, 23 percent moderate, 18 percent severe, and 2 percent severe with psychotic features. These data indicate that clinically depressed Filipino Americans tend to overuse non-psychiatric medical outpatient clinics. The data also confirm other studies indicating that Asian Americans underuse the mental health system, a practice that results in greater severity of disorders (Sue and Sue, 1974; Sue and McKinney, 1975). Nielsen and Williams (1980) have found that, in spite of the high prevalence of depression in medical settings, primary care physicians failed to diagnose depression 50 percent of the time. Moffic and Paykel's study (1975) of medical inpatients indicates that medical staff recognized depression in only 4 percent of their sample patients, although the rate of depression was determined by objective criteria to be 28.3 percent. Overall, the high prevalence of clinical or major depression, as shown in this study, also supports a California study reporting that only 20 percent of Filipino Americans, versus 32 percent of the total population, rated their lives as good (Cabezas, 1982).

Depression in Medical and Psychiatric Inpatient Units

The inpatient psychiatric units had the highest prevalence of severe cases with psychotic features (17.4 percent) but the lowest prevalence (26.1 percent) of major depression. The most common diagnosis upon admission of Filipino Americans to psychiatric units was schizophrenia (35 percent), followed by affective disorders (34 percent), major depression (26 percent), and bipolar disorder (8.0 percent).

Manifestations

Table 2.2 summarizes the clinical manifestations of a major depressive episode. The data were compiled after a number of participants were excluded from the various settings on the basis of our exclusion criteria, which included organic mental disorders, malignancies, AIDS, mental retardation, and such other psychiatric disorders as schizophrenia and bipolar disorders. Cases where organic factors may have triggered or maintained the cluster of symptoms (depressive syndrome) were also excluded. Completion rates for participants in the community, outpatient, and medical and psychiatric inpatient settings, after exclusions, were 80 percent, 65 percent, 78 percent, and 90 percent, respectively. The psychiatric inpatients had the highest completion rate because their interview sessions were conducted while these participants were still in the hospital.

Severity

Of the 39 clinically depressed participants identified in the community sample (n = 143), 14 (36 percent) and 15 (38 percent) had mild to moderate clinical or major depression, respectively. Usually, mild and moderate cases of clinical depression are not easily identified or recognized by clinicians who have not been trained specifically to identify depression among Filipino Americans. The majority of the symptoms of depression, such as dysphoric mood and cognitive and motivational symptoms, were described in the participants' native language. It was apparently easier for the participants to describe their symptoms this way; the interviewer, a Filipino physician, spoke their language and was perceived as someone who could easily understand them. The severe cases, with and without psychotic features, comprised 26 percent of the total of 39 clinically depressed participants in the community sample, with 10 percent of the severe cases (2.6 percent of the clinically depressed community sample) showing psychotic features.

In the outpatient clinic sample, 9 (17 percent) and 23 (44 percent) out of a total of 52 clinically depressed participants had mild or moderate depression, respectively. Of these cases, 38 percent were severe, with 10 percent of the severe cases exhibiting psychotic features, as the community sample, constituting 3.8 percent of the clinically depressed cases in the outpatient clinic sample.

In the medical inpatient sample, 23 percent, 35 percent, and 42 percent of the total of 26 clinically depressed participants had mild, moderate, or severe forms, respectively, with 9 percent of the severe cases showing psychotic features. Of the 12 clinically depressed participants in the psychiatric inpatient sample, all had severe cases, with 66.7 percent exhibiting psychotic features. This finding confirms previous studies showing that Asian Americans tend to have more severe depression when they are admitted to psychiatric units (Brown and others, 1973).

Measures of Depression

Mean scores on the depression scales, according to severity of the clinical depression (major depression), are shown in Table 2.3. The overall mean scores, regardless of severity, were 33.9 for the HRSD (Hamilton Rating Scale of Depression), 21.2 for the CES-D, and 13.1 for the BDI (Beck Depression Inventory). These scores invite comparison with scores for other minority groups. For example, Muñoz (1990) reported a CES-D mean score of 20.1 for the medical outpatient samples of Asian, Hispanic, and African American participants in a depression-prevention research project, a score comparable to our mean score of 21.2. For the BDI mean score, Muñoz reported 15.5 in the same sample; our mean score was 13.1.

Table 2.2. Symptoms and Clinical Features of Major Depressive Syndrome: Frequency and Severity Among Depressed and Nondepressed Participants.

	Nondepressed (*n* = 78)	*Mildly Depressed* (*n* = 24)	*Moderately Depressed* (*n* = 39)	*Severely Depressed* (*n* = 35)	*Depressed with Psychotic Features* (*n* = 12)
Affective Symptoms					
Depressed mood	59%	71%	92%	95%	91%
Irritability and anger	27%	38%	75%	65%	82%
Shakiness or nervousness inside	48%	60%	82%	89%	100%
Motivational Symptoms					
Loss of interest in things	19%	37%	60%	72%	83%
Feelings of hopelessness or helplessness	10%	22%	40%	63%	83%
Vegetative Symptoms					
Weight changes					
Weight loss (anorexia)	23%	55%	68%	70%	73%
Weight gain (overeating)	51%	46%	32%	30%	27%
Sleep changes					
Insomnia	47%	63%	70%	94%	92%
Trouble falling asleep	48%	87%	81%	89%	92%
Restless or disturbed sleep	47%	87%	81%	89%	92%
Early-morning awakening	54%	70%	73%	89%	92%
Hypersomnia (oversleeping)	5%	25%	15%	3%	3%
Psychomotor changes					
Agitation	25%	32%	60%	75%	83%
Retardation	67%	75%	90%	89%	92%
Fatigue	43%	67%	68%	93%	100%
Decreased libido (decreased interest in sex)	41%	50%	64%	80%	90%

Cognitive Symptoms					
Feelings of worthlessness	6%	26%	53%	66%	84%
Excessive or inappropriate guilt	42%	63%	69%	69%	71%
Feeling hopeless	10%	22%	40%	63%	83%
Worrying too much	74%	83%	95%	97%	92%
Diminished ability to think or concentrate	44%	62%	84%	85%	96%
Indecisiveness	44%	70%	84%	84%	85%
Memory problems	66%	83%	82%	94%	82%
Feeling crazy, or suspecting that something is wrong with one's mind	8%	11%	27%	48%	73%
Recurrent thoughts of death, or suicidal ideation	7%	11%	16%	50%	30%
Suicide attempt	—	—	—	14%	8%
Suicide	—	—	—	—	—
Somatic Symptoms					
Headaches	60%	76%	74%	77%	73%
Body weakness	38%	57%	76%	82%	82%
Chest pains	45%	65%	68%	64%	82%
Heavy feeling in extremities	36%	65%	65%	71%	75%
Upset stomach or nausea	42%	47%	67%	73%	67%
Dizziness or faintness	40%	43%	53%	85%	73%
Cold or hot spells	24%	42%	54%	70%	70%
Muscle soreness	61%	86%	78%	79%	83%
Tingling or numbness in body parts	40%	40%	66%	61%	73%
Trouble catching one's breath	14%	23%	49%	65%	60%
Lump in throat	9%	12%	30%	48%	45%
Pains in the lower back	59%	67%	69%	66%	82%

Note: Symptoms and severity are based on the revised third edition of the *Diagnostic and Statistical Manual of Mental Disorders (DSM III-R)* (American Psychiatric Association, 1987) and on the symptom checklist of Derogatis (1973).

Table 2.3. Mean Scores on Depression Scales Among Filipino Americans by Severity of Major Depression.

	HRSD[a]	*BDI*[b]	*CES-D*[c]
Severity of Depression[d]			
Mild	17.6	7.0	13.4
Moderate	28.7	14.8	19.9
Severe	40.1	26.2	25.9
With psychotic features	49.3	26.2	25.7

[a]Hamilton Rating Scale for Depression (Hamilton, 1960).
[b]Beck Depression Inventory (Beck and others, 1961).
[c]Scale developed for the Center for Epidemiological Studies (Radloff, 1977).
[d]Severity is measured according to the criteria listed in the revised third edition of the *Diagnostic and Statistical Manual of Mental Disorders (DSM III-R)* (American Psychiatric Association, 1987).

Significant depressive symptoms are summarized in Table 2.4. Aside from the common vegetative and somatic symptoms, clinically depressed Filipino Americans showed significant cognitive, affective, and motivational symptoms. Such nonsomatic symptoms were usually described once the participants had started to trust the interviewer, or when they perceived that they could be helped with their problems, whether these were medical and psychiatric problems or psychosocial problems, like unemployment.

In our study, we found that Filipino Americans tended to minimize their symptoms when self-administered measures were used. For instance, mean scores of severely depressed participants in various subcategories of the Symptom Checklist-90 (SLC-90) were less than 2, but many of their self-described "moderate" symptoms were found to be severe when the participants were personally interviewed.

Affective Symptoms

The affective symptoms shown in Table 2.2 were rarely the reasons why the clinically depressed participants consulted physicians or sought other help. In this study, a direct question ("How

Table 2.4. Common Symptoms of Clinical Depression Among Filipino Americans ($n = 110$).

	Kendall's Tau B Correlation Coefficients	*P-value*
Affective Symptoms		
Feeling easily annoyed or irritated	.34	.001
Nervousness or shakiness inside	.45	.0001
Feeling lonely	.35	.001
Crying easily	.44	.0001
Feeling blue or sad	.45	.0001
Feeling fearful	.39	.001
Having temper outbursts one cannot control	.34	.004
Vegetative Symptoms		
Feeling low on energy or slowed down	.36	.0001
Having sleep that is restless or disturbed	.41	.0001
Having trouble falling asleep	.38	.0003
Feeling that everything is an effort	.44	.0001
Awakening in the early morning	.47	.0001
Loss of sexual interest or pleasure	.30	.009
Poor appetite	.30	.008
Feeling pushed to get things done	.42	.003
Motivational Symptoms		
Difficulty making decisions	.43	.0002
Feelings of worthlessness	.41	.001
Thoughts of death or dying	.26	.028
Feelings of inferiority to others	.25	.04
Feelings of hopelessness about the future	.35	.004
Cognitive Symptoms		
Worrying too much about things	.50	.0001
Having trouble remembering things	.33	.002
Getting one's feelings easily hurt	.40	.002
Having persistent unwanted thoughts, words, or ideas in one's mind	.49	.0001
Feeling that people will take advantage if one lets them	.29	.01
Feeling guilt	.29	.008
Having trouble concentrating	.47	.0001
Thinking that something is seriously wrong with one's body	.36	.001
Feeling that others do not understand one	.30	.009
Having ideas or beliefs that others do not share	.40	.002
Somatic Symptoms		
Headaches	.27	.01
Weakness in parts of one's body	.37	.001
Heart pounding or racing	.21	.05
Pains in heart or chest	.28	.01

Table 2.4. Common Symptoms of Clinical Depression Among Filipino Americans ($n = 110$), Cont'd.

	Kendall's Tau B Correlation Coefficients	*P-value*
Dizziness or faintness	.196	.08
Nausea or upset stomach	.28	.017
Heavy feeling in arms and legs	.35	.004
Numbness or tingling in parts of one's body	.24	.05
Hot and cold spells	.31	.011
Trouble catching one's breath	.31	.014

Note: The symptoms listed here were elicited using the Symptom Checklist–90 (Derogatis, Lipunan, and Covi, 1973).

have you been feeling?") was not asked at the start; instead, questions like "What has bothered you a lot?" and "What have you been worried or thinking about?" were asked initially. The participants usually answered by relating their immediate concerns, such as unemployment, or such somatic complaints as headaches and body weakness.

After they were allowed to express their immediate concerns, patients usually expressed their feelings, generally in their native language or dialect, especially when they were asked in the native language, "Ano ang pakiramdam ninyo?" ("How do you feel?") Nearly 60 percent of the participants expressed dysphoric mood by saying, "Masama ang pakiramdam ko" ("I am not feeling well") or "Masama ang loob ko" ("I feel hurt and/or sad"). They expressed anger or irritability by saying, "Palaging mainit ang ulo ko," which literally means "my head is always hot." They described feelings of anxiety by saying, "Nanginginig ang loob ko" (literally, "I feel cold"). Anxiety was also described as *nerbyos,* nervousness inside or shakiness; 100 percent of the participants with psychotic depression complained of feeling nervous or shaky inside.

Araneta (1993) reports that the characteristic symptoms of major depressive disorders are not recognized easily among Filipino Americans because these symptoms are masked by panic attacks. He postulates that depression, which could be perceived as a form of punishment and as a sign of weak character, may be seen as a stigma, which precipitates a panic that masks depressive symptoms. The majority of our Filipino American participants both from the depressed and the normal groups were smiling while they talked about serious problems or reported sad, hurt, or angry feelings. Some went from smiling to tears, or vice versa, in a very short time during the interview and usually asked forgiveness for crying: "Forgive me, I can't control myself." (A clinician not familiar with this kind of smiling among Filipino Americans might label it "inappropriate affect.") But after the participants started to trust the interviewer or clinician, or once they perceived the latter as somebody who understood them and could help with their immediate problems, their affect became congruent with their real moods and concerns.

> Vignette. *During the initial interview, Mrs. S. was asked what had been bothering her recently. She responded by saying,* "Doctora *(*referring to a female doctor*),* wala akong trabaho" *("Doctor, I don't have a job"). While she told the sad story of how she had lost her job, Mrs. S. was smiling.*
>
> *She said that she had quit her job when she became ill. She recalled that she frequently had felt tired, complaining of weakness of the extremities accompanied by insomnia, poor appetite, and loss of weight for four to five weeks. She also had felt discouraged about her failing health and her loss of interest in her work, and so she resigned from her job.*
>
> *Upon further inquiry, she revealed that she had been feeling very worried, hurt, and angry with her husband, who was having an affair with a coworker. She felt betrayed after all her sacrifices for him. (She had saved a lot of money in order to sponsor him in coming to the United States and support him until he found a job.) Toward the end of the interview, crying, she expressed frustration, intense anger, and feelings of belittlement in her native dialect. She also said that she planned to file for*

divorce, but she did not have a lawyer and could not afford one. She was becoming more worried about her worsening financial situation, and she asked for advice about going back to work. She also asked for a referral to a good lawyer.

Motivational Symptoms

Regardless of severity, 63 percent of the clinically depressed participants reported loss of interest in things (*nawalan ng gana*), compared to 19 percent of the nondepressed group. This symptom of depression can lead to serious consequences, such as loss of a job or inability to look for work. Unemployment and its ill effects "double" the depression, resulting in still more serious problems for patients and their families.

Feelings of hopelessness were least commonly reported by mildly and moderately depressed participants but were more common among the severely depressed. Loss of interest in sex can also jeopardize a marriage or a relationship and may result in separation, divorce, or conflicts. Therefore, it is important not to conclude too quickly that a divorce or a separation has precipitated clinical depression in a divorced or separated patient. It is possible that the symptoms of depression may have led to the divorce or separation.

Vignette. *Ms. M. was a forty-eight-year-old Filipino American who claimed to be "madly in love" with her younger, good-looking, twenty-nine-year-old Irish American immigrant husband. They had been married for about six years. (Ms. M. had divorced her first husband, whom she had married "just to come to the United States.")*

Ms. M. reported having felt betrayed by her first husband, who had sent her a photo of a young man while she was still in the Philippines, claiming that it was his picture. He wanted to marry her immediately. When she went to Hawaii to marry him, she found out that he was seventy years old.

*She felt obligated (*utang na loob*) to marry him because he had paid her fare to the United States. After she had repaid her "debt," she divorced him.*

She then went to California and met her present husband. She decided to marry him in spite of their age difference. Her present husband was very loving, and she could not have hoped for more in the relationship.

About two months before her interview, however, she began to experience irritability accompanied by insomnia, anorexia, chronic fatigue, crying spells for no reason, and decreased libido for more than three months. She claimed that she had completely lost interest in sex, for no apparent reason. She also felt that she wanted to divorce her husband, also for no good reason. During the interview, she cried and expressed feelings of guilt because her mind "told" her to divorce her husband, but she knew that this was very irrational, because they loved each other.

She had been in the process of filing for divorce when her family doctor, who had not found any physical problems, advised her to consult a psychiatrist, who subsequently diagnosed her as having clinical depression.

She was told that loss of interest in sex is one of the symptoms of depression. She felt very relieved to hear that depression is an illness, and that her symptoms were part of the illness. Knowing that she had an illness, she cooperated with the treatment of her depression and did not pursue her divorce plans. She responded well to antidepressant medicine and to individual psychotherapy.

Cognitive Symptoms

Too much worrying, memory problems, poor attention span, decreased concentration, and indecisiveness were the most common cognitive symptoms; 27 percent of all the clinically depressed participants reported recurrent thoughts of death or suicidal ideation, and those who were severely depressed without psychotic features reported the highest (50 percent) suicidal ideation and attempts (12 percent). The majority of suicidal ideation was passive. For instance, an elderly man prayed that God would take him, and he asked for surgery for his cardiac problem, hoping that he would die during the surgery. No suicide was reported during the study, however.

> **Vignette.** *Mr. T., a fifty-nine-year-old Filipino American accountant, described feeling stress because of work overload and pressure. He said he had not felt well for the past five months. He had not been sleeping well for about two months. It took him a long time to get to sleep, and then he would wake up around 2 A.M. and could not go back to sleep. He did not feel like eating and had lost about eight pounds. He had enjoyed gardening and dancing before, but now he seemed to have lost interest in everything. Upon further inquiry, he revealed that he had also lost interest in having sex with his wife. He complained of very poor concentration and poor memory: "I can't read the newspaper. I can't remember what I've read on the previous page. I also forget my car keys, and I leave the car without turning off the engine."*
>
> *The immediate precipitant of his depressive symptoms was a problem with his job and his supervisor. He felt that he had been discriminated against when he did not get the promotion he wanted after working for about seven years; instead, a younger employee was promoted and was now his supervisor. He complained that his new supervisor put too much pressure on him. For example, when he was tying his shoes, the supervisor shouted at him, "You're not working! You're just relaxing!" When this happened, he felt like strangling the man. He*

decided to stop working because he was afraid that he might not be able to control himself and might actually kill his supervisor. He also felt so bad about himself that he planned to jump from a high building, but he thought that this was contrary to his religion (he was a Roman Catholic). He felt very irritable, sad, and worried, and at times confused. He had diarrhea on and off and stomachaches that he claimed were due to stress.

About eight years ago, he had experienced similar symptoms related to his job and had also felt discriminated against. He had been suicidal and was hospitalized. He responded to antidepressant medication and to psychotherapy for one year.

This patient was the eldest of eight siblings. His father, a strict disciplinarian who administered physical punishment, had died when the patient was twelve, and his mother had remarried when he was seventeen. He considered himself diligent and magaling *(good). He had held two jobs (accountant and rest-home manager) for many years. He was also worried about his wife, a vocational nurse, who recently had suffered a back injury in an accident, and about his youngest son, a "spoiled brat" who had failed in high school and was not able to graduate.*

The patient was admitted to a psychiatric ward and, once again, responded well to antidepressant medication. He had been hesitant initially to be admitted, but he decided to let himself be confined when he learned that a Filipino doctor was available to see him, answer questions, and allay his fears about hospitalization.

Suicide

As already mentioned, none of the participants in our study committed suicide. Suicide attempts were most common among nonpsychotic severely depressed participants. Of the 35 nonpsychotic severely depressed participants, 4 (12 percent) attempted suicide, whereas only 1 out of the 12 psychotic severely depressed participants tried to kill himself. None of the mildly and moderately depressed participants attempted suicide. Most of those who did attempt suicide were females. Many of them claimed that they had not really planned these attempts, and later they expressed remorse.

Comparisons with other Asian American groups may be useful. In San Francisco's Chinatown, the suicide rate was 27.9 per 100,000 in the period from 1952 to 1968, a rate about three times higher than the general U.S. rate of 10 per 100,000, with suicide among Chinese men four to five times more frequent than among Chinese women (Bourne, 1973). Barbiturate overdose was the most frequent method. In Japanese culture, suicide is considered an honorable method of dying, and death by *hara-kiri* is associated with the ruling class in the feudal system. Nevertheless, rate of suicide among Japanese Americans has not been found to be significantly greater than that of other minority groups (Fujii, Fukushima and Yamamoto, 1993). There was a difference, however, in the suicide methods used by acculturated and nonacculturated Japanese Americans in Los Angeles. The acculturated Japanese Americans overdosed on drugs or shot themselves, whereas the nonacculturated group frequently used hanging, jumping, suffocation, and wrist slashing, all considered "more Japanese" (Yamamoto, 1976).

A study conducted in Manila at the Philippine General Hospital (Ignacio, 1991) shows that 0.2 percent of the medical emergency cases brought to the hospital within a one-year period were suicidal patients and constituted about one-third of all emergency psychiatric referrals. This study reports that more females than males, and mostly single females, attempted suicide. The majority were first attempts. Only one patient died, after ingesting hydrochloric acid, a common household antiseptic in the Philippines. This study also reports that poisoning was the most common method, with subjects ingesting insecticides and INH (isoniazid), an antituberculosis medication readily available without prescription. Most of the suicide attempts in Manila were impulsive; 50 percent of the patients thought of killing themselves within only a few hours or days of experiencing their stressors. But whereas the attempts were impulsive, the methods were particularly lethal.

In our study, overdosing on nonprescription drugs (such as cold medications) and sleeping pills was the most common method, and suicidal ideas were passive. One patient planned to shoot himself but did not pursue his plans because he could not afford to buy a gun. Another man, who had been a successful accountant in the Philippines but was not able to practice his profession in the United States, wanted to commit suicide but, after computing the cost of his burial, decided not to kill himself.

Vegetative Symptoms

Of the vegetative symptoms, insomnia and fatigue or loss of energy were reported by more than 90 percent of the severely depressed participants; weight gain or overeating and hypersomnia were more commonly observed in mild depression. As shown in Table 2.2, overeating and hypersomnia decreased as depression became more severe. These symptoms may be compensatory mechanisms at the early stage of depression. A common belief regarding decreased libido, usually reported by postmenopausal women, was that sex after menopause is a sin or may cause cancer.

Other Clinical Observations

Another physician once asked one of us, "Is depression common among Filipinos? They always look happy." It is common for Filipinos, depressed or not, to smile even when relating sad events or reporting hurt feelings. But this so-called nervous smile should not be taken at face value, and clinicians should not be misled into believing that the Filipino patient is not depressed. When Filipinos in our study expressed their sad or angry feelings, they usually asked for forgiveness as if the expression of feelings were wrong. This behavior is fostered by some Filipino child-rearing practices, which do not allow the expression of negative feelings to parents or authority figures.

Three clinically depressed participants reported homicidal ideation. They wanted to kill their work supervisors when they felt harassed or discriminated against or when scolded or shamed in front of others. Participants sometimes asked the interviewer personal questions, usually in the second or third interview session, especially when rapport had been established. For example, they asked, "Are you married? Do you have children? Which part of the Philippines are you from?" They usually expected direct and honest answers. In psychotherapy sessions conducted by strict psychoanalysts, who tend not to answer personal questions, such direct questions will not be answered, and the Filipino patient may feel rejected or unable to connect with the therapist, which may lead to early termination of therapy.

Asked what depression as a mental health problem meant to them, the participants gave answers (shown in Table 2.5) that reflected their understanding of this problem. Forty-nine percent of the participants did not know or understand what depression is, while 51 percent expressed some understanding of the problem. The most common equivalent native-language words for *depressed* were *sad* and *worried,* accounting for 29 percent of responses, followed by *hopeless* (11 percent), *with a lot of problems* (4 percent), and *unaccomplished* (3 percent). Other terms and phrases were *confused, irritable, crazy, looks tired and sad, lowering of social status, hurt feelings,* and *financial difficulties.* Of the 110 clinically depressed participants, 75 percent did not consider their depression to be a pressing health problem and did not ask for professional help. But 77.8 percent of those who considered physical and medical complaints (arthritis, peptic ulcer, hypertension, and diabetes) to be pressing health problems were found to be clinically depressed, with varying severity (mostly mild to moderate). More than 65 percent of the participants who presented themselves as having suffered some sort of "nervous breakdown" were found to have major depression, and almost all those who considered "sadness" or "depression" to be their major health problem were found to be clinically depressed. Of those who were diagnosed with major depression, 25.4 percent were not aware of or denied the disorder. Exhibit 2.1 gives an overview of medical conditions that can cause depressive symptoms.

Table 2.5. Participants' Understanding of What It Means to Be "Depressed."

Native-Language Word or Phrase	*Close English Equivalent*	*Percentage Responding*
Walang sagot; Hindi alam	(No answer given)	49
Malungkot; Naguol	Sad; lonely; worried	29
Walang pag-asa	Hopeless	11
Maraming problema	Having a lot of problems	4
Walang nagawa para sa sarili	Unaccomplished	3
Nalilito	Confused	4
Aburido	Irritable	4
Masyadong inaasahan ng iba	Under pressure	4
Walang kapanatagan	Feel insecure	4
Awa sa sarili	Self-pity	4
Kulang ang tiwala sa sarili	Feeling inferior; lacking self-confidence	4
Nabubuhay sa nakaraan	Living in the past	4
Inaapi	Being treated badly	4
Sinisisi ang ibang tao sa kanilang kahirapan	Blaming others for difficulties	4
Naloloko	Going crazy	4
Nagagalit	Getting angry	4
Matamlay	Looking tired and sad	4
Maramdamin	Sensitive	4
Walang mapagsabihan ng sama ng loob	Having no one to talk to	4
Hindi kayang lutasin ang problema	Not being able to solve problems	4
Bumaba ang katayuan sa buhay	Lowering of social status	4
Walang pera o nahihirapan sa pera	Having financial difficulties	4
Masama ang loob	Having hurt feelings	4
Nag-aalala	Worrying	4
Nahiubos; Mahiobsanon	Feeling hurt; getting easily hurt	4

Conclusion

This study shows that the prevalence of clinical depression is higher among Filipino Americans than in the general U.S. population. As shown by the various depression measures that were utilized, Filipino Americans have cognitive, affective, and motivational symptoms in addition to the usual vegetative and somatic complaints commonly reported by studies of other Asian populations (Cheung, Law, and Waldman, 1980–81; Kleinman,

Exhibit 2.1. A Medical Overview of Depression.

Medical and Organic Conditions That Can Cause Symptoms of Clinical Depression and Other Psychiatric Disorders

It is not uncommon for symptoms of clinical depression to be among the earliest signs of such medical illnesses as cancer (for example, pancreatic cancer) and hypothyroidism before the full-blown signs and symptoms of the disease appear. Early detection and treatment of medical disorders that cause depression is very important. A number of common disorders are commonly called the "great mimickers of psychiatry" (Gold, 1986) because psychiatric symptoms like depression and anxiety are among their clinical presentations. They include the following:

Thyroid Disease

Hypothyroidism. This is a very common neuroendocrine disorder, especially among women and those who live in the mountain provinces of the Philippines, where sources of iodine (such as seafoods) are scarce. It is a condition caused by a decrease in the secretion of thyroid hormone by the thyroid gland. Drugs like lithium are known to cause hypothyroidism.

Hypothyroidism is the most common medical illness that has a clinical presentation of depression, together with cold intolerance, bradycardia (slowing of heart rate), fatigue, delayed reflexes, brittle hair, goiter (enlargement of thyroid gland), dry and thickened skin, weight gain, and cardiac failure. Myxedema is a severe form of hypothyroidism, which may start early in life. It is characterized by the above signs and symptoms and by puffy, dull-looking and drooping eyelids, enlarged heart, hoarse voice, increased menstrual flow, and sparse hair.

Hyperthyroidism (Graves' Disease). This is considered to be a genetic autoimmune illness, common among women between the ages of twenty to forty. Graves' disease is a result of increased secretion of thyroid hormone, causing increased metabolic rate. Depression is also a common symptom of this condition, accompanied by excessive sweating, restlessness, fine tremors of the hands, muscular weakness, exophthalmus (protrusion of eyeballs), extreme heat sensitivity, moist skin, irritability, heart palpitations, anxiety, mood swings, diarrhea, and increased appetite. Thyroid crisis or "storm" may occur abruptly after surgery, extreme fright, severe physical stress, abrupt discontinuance of antihyperthyroid drugs, and complications of pregnancy (for example, toxemia) and diabetes (for example, shock). This condition can be fatal if not treated promptly. Its clinical presentation may also include psychosis, fever, confusion, and shock.

Adrenal Disease

Addison's Disease. This rare condition is due to the failure of the adrenal cortex to secrete such hormones as aldosterone (responsible for maintaining increased sodium and decreased potassium levels in the blood) and glucocorticoids, which

Exhibit 2.1. A Medical Overview of Depression, Cont'd.

---

assist in maintaining blood sugar and help alleviate the effects of stress and allergy and fight infection. This disease is characterized by symptoms of depression, apathy, sleepiness or insomnia, fatigue, low blood pressure, weakness, shortness of breath, darkening skin and, at times, lowering of blood sugar, nausea, dizziness, sensitivity to cold, and anorexia. Addison's crisis (severe failure of the adrenal cortex) is characterized by extreme pain in the abdomen, lower back, and legs, as well as vascular and kidney failure.

Cushing's Disease or Syndrome. This disorder is caused by overactivity of the adrenal cortex, due to tumors in the adrenals or elsewhere in the body that secrete a hormone (ACTH) that stimulates the adrenal cortex. Cushing's syndrome includes presentations of clinical depression, anxiety, manic depression, psychosis, "dulling of the intellect," fat deposits ("buffalo lump"), acne, hirsutism in women, weight gain, high blood pressure, menstrual problems, osteoperosis, diabetes, impairment in wound healing, and easy bruising.

Parathyroid Disease

Hypoparathyroidism. The parathyroid glands secrete less parathyroid hormone, which results in decreased calcium in the blood (hypocalcemia), accompanied by depression, anxiety, irritability, weakness, muscular spasm, and, in severe cases, psychosis and dementia. Hypoparathyroidism is at times caused by thyroid surgery, when the parathyroid glands, located behind the thyroid, are inadvertently removed by the surgeon.

Hyperparathyroidism. This condition is caused by parathyroid tumors, which increase secretions of parathyroid hormone, leading to hypercalcemia (increased blood calcium). Clinical depression also develops with hypercalcemia, together with delusions, hallucinations, confusion, and personality changes in chronic and severe cases.

Diabetes Mellitus

This disorder is due to underproduction or nonproduction of insulin by the pancreas, resulting in increased blood sugar. Early onset (under age thirty) diabetes (Type I, insulin-dependent) and late onset (over age 30) diabetes (Type II, non–insulin-dependent) can cause symptoms of major depression, together with extreme thirst, frequent urination, hunger, weight loss, lethargy, delayed healing of wounds, frequent infections, and blindness. Moderate to severe diabetes can lead to impotence, stroke, and kidney failure.

Hypoglycemia (decreased blood sugar) can occur during treatment of diabetes or may be due to overdose of insulin and, in some cases, to tumors in the pancreas that secrete insulin. Clinically, hypoglycemia can cause depressive symptoms, together with severe hunger, nervousness or shakiness, fainting spells, weak-

Exhibit 2.1. A Medical Overview of Depression, Cont'd.

---

ness, headaches, blurry vision, and, in severe cases, unconsciousness, convulsions, and coma. Moderate and less severe chronic hypoglycemia can cause slurred speech, confusion, anxiety, "drunk appearance," paranoid disorder, and manifestations that mimic schizophrenia and dementia.

Pheochromocytoma

These are benign tumors of the adrenal medulla and other parts of the body that secrete norepinephrine and epinephrine, causing high blood pressure. The condition commonly occurs at an early age (five to twenty-five). These tumors can cause clinical depression and anxiety in severe cases, with psychotic features. There are commonly paniclike attacks characterized by headache, dizziness, shakiness, increased heart rate, dyspnea, throat tightness, nausea, weakness, chest pains, and tingling sensations in the arms and legs. The attacks may occur during severe emotional stress. They can also be precipitated by coitus, pregnancy, straining, urinating, laughing, sneezing, and hyperventilation.

Guidelines for Intervention

1. Clinical depression and medical illness may coexist coincidentally but are not necessarily related. In patients with affective disorders, there is a high rate of medical illnesses that have very little or nothing to do with the affective disorders. It is a challenge to the attending physician to know what is causing which symptom.
2. Medical or physical illness can cause symptoms of depression. For example, the endocrine disorders (such as hypothyroidism) are common physical causes of depressive symptoms. Treatment of these medical causes is mandatory in order to treat the depression.
3. Medical illness can aggravate clinical depression. An existing medical illness (such as chronic and debilitating conditions like kidney disease or diabetes) can cause emotional stress and make a superimposed depression worse. The high rate of relapse and nonresponse to psychiatric treatment may be due to underlying, untreated medical illness.
4. Depression can develop in response to an existing medical illness (such as AIDS) or after heart surgery. Some patients recover from their depression once they become adjusted to their medical conditions.
5. Depressogenic life events, such as loss of loved ones or unemployment, may precipitate illness or predispose a person to physical illnesses like cancer and hypertension. There is also increasing evidence that depression affects the immune system, a circumstance that may lead to the development of medical illnesses.
6. Medications for medical illnesses—antihypertensive drugs, steroids, and some antiulcer medications—may cause depression.

1978). The rate (0.98 percent) of suicidal attempts or plans is much lower in this study, however, than in comparable studies of the general population (Sue and Morishima, 1982). This finding may be explained in part by the fact that Filipino Americans are predominantly Catholic and may consider suicide a mortal sin.

The cognitive, affective, and motivational symptoms could be better predictors of clinical depression among Filipino Americans, especially in medical outpatient and inpatient settings, than somatic and vegetative symptoms, which may be hard to differentiate from symptoms secondary to physical illness. Moreover, these cognitive, affective, and motivational symptoms were described when participants were asked about them in their native language or dialect and when they trusted the interviewer or perceived the interviewer as being able to understand their feelings and problems.

The majority of the clinically depressed participants in community and medical outpatient settings were either mildly or moderately depressed. This finding may imply that depression, if detected early, will respond more quickly to intervention.

Chapter 3

Psychosociocultural Profiles

The significant role of psychosocial and cultural factors in prevention, development, treatment, and intervention with mental disorders has been recognized (Marsella, 1980; Kleinman, 1982; Billings and Moos, 1982). In the conceptualization of the causes and treatments of mental illness, the biomedical model was challenged to include psychosocial and cultural aspects. The biopsychosocial model was proposed because "the boundaries between health and disease, between well and sick, are far from clear and never will be clear, for they are confused by cultural, social and psychological considerations" (Engel, 1977). Such considerations must be investigated, particularly among minority groups and immigrants.

In response to the growing demand for more information on Filipino Americans, the study described in Chapter Two was undertaken. The study gathered data on psychosocial and cultural factors associated with clinically depressed (CD) and nondepressed (ND) Filipino Americans from several settings. Clinical depression, considered the "common cold" of mental health, was studied among Filipino Americans because, as indicated by previous studies (Kuo, 1984), any minority population that has experienced significant socioenvironmental stressors will be likely to have a higher prevalence of mental health problems (such as depression) than will the general population.

Since Filipino Americans are a minority group and are mostly immigrants, it can be assumed that they have experienced various types of stressors, such as unmet expectations, unemployment or underemployment, legal and immigration problems, separation from and absence of social support, and cultural and adjustment problems that drain their physical, social, and mental resources.

As indicated by our study, Filipino Americans do indeed have a higher prevalence of clinical depression than does the general population. Many of them will need help in overcoming depression, and so clinicians must have thorough knowledge of their psychosociocultural profile in order to plan culturally appropriate treatment and intervention and prevent high-risk individuals from developing severe depression. Previous studies have identified psychosocial factors, such as stressful life events and stress-buffering factors, that are important in the development and treatment of depression (Paykel, 1974; Dean and Lin, 1977). Psychosociocultural factors that are of great interest to clinicians include clients' and their families' conceptualization and beliefs about the causes of mental illness, as well as their awareness of their own mental health problems, expressions of and reactions to mental illness, and preferred modes and types of treatment; cultural background of the therapist; clients' cultural values, goals, and expectations as well as their family, immigration, and work histories; the number and types of stressors; networks of social support; and clients' coping skills, personality traits, and childhood and adolescent histories.

A psychosocial interview protocol and a questionnaire were developed (with Pilipino/Tagalog translation) and pretested specifically for our study. It included a demographic profile; immigration, family, and work history; expectation and goals; stressors; coping resources and skills; concepts and beliefs; and childhood and adolescent history. Important findings of the study will be highlighted in this chapter.

The psychosociocultural profile of clinically depressed Filipino American participants did not differ significantly from setting to setting. This was also true of nondepressed participants from the various settings. Since there were no significant differences among the clinically depressed participants from the various settings, their psychosociocultural profiles were combined, and their data were compared with the combined data for the nondepressed group. There were 110 clinically depressed participants who met the criteria for a major depressive episode, as well as 78 nondepressed, control participants who completed face-to-face interview sessions. Many participants expressed their feelings in Tagalog or Cebuano.

Sociodemographic Profile

Table 3.1 summarizes the sociodemographic profile of the clinically depressed and nondepressed Filipino Americans.

Gender

There were more females (65 percent) among the participants, reflecting the gender distribution of recent Filipino immigrants to the United States, but there were no significant differences between the CD and ND groups on gender. This finding is contrary to the usual finding in the United States that the prevalence of depression is about two times greater in women than in men.

Age, Place of Birth, and Subethnic Group

The two groups did not differ significantly on average age (forty-seven) or age of arrival in the United States (thirty-five), place of birth (97 percent were Philippine-born), or subethnic group. However, fewer Ilocanos tended to be depressed: 20.5 percent of them were nondepressed, and only 8.2 percent were found to be clinically depressed. Tagalogs, Visayans, and other subethnic groups were almost equally distributed between the depressed and nondepressed groups. Why the Ilocanos had less of a tendency to become depressed needs to be studied. They are known

Table 3.1. Demographic Profile of Clinically Depressed and Nondepressed Filipino Americans.

	Clinically Depressed (CD) (n = 110)		*Nondepressed (ND) (n = 78)*	
Characteristics	*Number*	*Percentage*	*Number*	*Percentage*
Sex				
Male	39	35.5	27	34.6
Female	71	64.5	51	65.4
Age (mean years, *SD*)	(46.1,	±16.3)	(47.6,	±14.7)
Place of birth				
Philippines	105	95.5	76	97.4
U.S.	5	4.5	2	2.6
Subethnic group				
Tagalog	53	48.2	32	41.0
Visayan	32	29.1	19	24.4
Ilocano	9	8.2	16	20.5
Other	16	14.5	11	14.1
Religion				
Roman Catholic	97	88.2	67	85.9
Protestant	3	2.7	3	3.8
Other	10	9.1	8	10.3
Practicing religion[a]				
Yes	75	71.4	67	87.0
No	30	28.6	10	13.0
Employment status[b]				
Unemployed	52	47.3	12	15.4
Employed	58	52.7	66	84.6
Change of financial status[c]				
About the same	17	16.7	15	21.7
Better than last year	32	31.3	36	52.2
Worse than last year	53	52.0	18	26.1

[a]Significant difference between CD and ND groups ($p < 0.02$, Fisher's exact test, 2-tail).

[b]Significant difference between CD and ND groups ($p < 0.01$, Fisher's exact test, 2-tail.

[c]Significant difference between CD and ND groups ($\bar{x}^2 = 11.7$, $df = 2$, $p < 0.003$).

for their thrift and industry; perhaps they tend to be more financially stable, which could be a buffering factor against depression.

Religion, Education, and Financial Status

The majority (87 percent) of all the participants were Roman Catholic, a finding that reflects the home country's predominant religion, but there were significant differences on the practice of religion, regardless of type. Of the clinically depressed, 28.6 percent did not practice their religion, whereas 87 percent of the nondepressed group did practice. Practice of one's religion has been identified as a factor that may prevent or minimize the development of depression. Spiritual and religious beliefs, and the social aspects of religious activities, may also help mitigate depressive symptoms, and religious groups may provide emotional, spiritual, and material support to their depressed members. Why there were more clinically depressed participants who did not practice their religion has not been investigated. Perhaps the CD group was alienated from the usual social or religious support groups or may have been preoccupied with simply trying to survive.

Marital Status

The groups did not differ significantly on marital status, but among the CD group, 15.5 percent were divorced, while only 3.8 percent of the ND group was divorced. Divorce among Filipino American immigrants not only may be a severe stressor but also may be considered an extreme to catastrophic stressor, since divorce is not allowed by the Catholic Church and is illegal in the Philippines. Aside from the "ripple effects" of divorce, such as financial difficulties and problems with children, there is the feeling of shame, or *hiya:* the guilt and stigma associated with being divorced, not only among Filipino Americans but also back in the Philippines, once news of the divorce reaches home. Religious and social stigma, in addition to strong family values, may explain the lower divorce rate among Filipino Americans than in the general population of the United States.

The educational level of the participants also reflects the educational status of Filipino immigrants, who are predominantly college-educated (Bouvier and Martin, 1985). However, many of the Filipino immigrants could not get jobs commensurate with their educational status. The two groups differed significantly on present occupation, with the CD group having more semiskilled and unskilled jobs. The ND group had more professional jobs, with higher income. There was also significantly more unemployment in the CD group, and more of the CD participants reported significant worsening of financial status over the preceding year. Participants with individual or family income over $30,000 had a lower rate of clinical depression than low-income participants. More than 80 percent of the unemployed participants were found to have varying degrees of depression.

Immigration History

Among participants in both groups, 71 percent had arrived after 1972. The groups had no significant differences in visa and immigration status, but 85 percent of those found to have visa and immigration problems were clinically depressed, with varying severity. Many of them were overstaying Filipino tourists who worked illegally and had become victims of underemployment and of abuse by their employers. Some were forced to marry in order to change their visa status; a number had even paid their prospective spouses. For example, one overstaying tourist—a former teacher, married with five children and a husband in the Philippines—paid the son of her employer $3,000 to become her husband. After her marriage to this spouse-for-hire, he physically and sexually abused her and constantly harassed her for more money, threatening to report her to immigration officials if she did not comply. Some of the participants had arrived as "mail-order brides" or as pen pals of their prospective spouses, and many of these marriages were also reported to be short-lived or disastrous.

Family History

The two groups differed significantly on family history of depression, alcoholism, and other emotional or mental problems, as well as on spouse's nationality, living with children, and annual income. As shown in Table 3.2, the two groups also differed significantly on primary reason for coming to the United States. The majority had come to find a job or have a better life, but more than one-third (36.8 percent) of the ND group had come to join a spouse or family, while only 14.2 percent of the CD group had done so. There was a significant difference among mildly, moderately, and severely depressed participants on family history of depression, alcoholism, and other mental health problems. For instance, severely depressed participants with psychotic features had a 100 percent positive family history of depression; severely depressed participants without psychotic features, moderately depressed participants, and mildly depressed participants had a 44.4 percent, 22.5 percent, and 11.5 percent positive family history, respectively. The nondepressed group had only a 10.3 percent positive family history of depression and a 6.4 percent positive history of alcoholism. These data support theories of genetic or biological determinants associated with major depression and alcoholism.

More than one-fourth of the CD group had non-Filipino spouses, compared to 11.1 percent of the ND group. Cultural differences become a major issue in a mixed marriage, which may precipitate depression if the marriage fails. More of the ND group had their children living with them; many of the children of the CD group were still in the Philippines. As expected, the family annual income of the ND group was significantly higher than that of the CD group. It is a common practice among Filipino Americans to buy a house once the family has saved enough. Adult employed children or relatives are expected to contribute to the cost of the house. When children get married or have their own families, they may be allowed to stay in their parents' house until they are financially able to live on their own. Children are usually encouraged to finish their studies (and, preferably, earn a college degree) before they get married.

Work History, Expectations, and Goals

The two groups had similar work histories in the Philippines and encountered similar problems in the United States when looking for jobs (no local experience, no specific training for the job, too much competition, discrimination, no license). However, the CD group differed significantly from the ND group on problems with their current U.S. jobs.

Asked what they had expected to happen in the United States, the groups did not differ significantly in their responses. The majority in both groups sent money and other material goods to their relatives in the Philippines, as they had been expected to do once they had begun working in the United States.

Compared with the ND group, more of the CD participants reported their expectations as unrealized. Spouses' expectations were similar to the participants' and did not differ significantly between the CD and ND groups. Again, more CD participants reported their spouses' expectations as unrealized. Aside from personal expectations, both groups had similar family (nuclear and extended) expectations, but more (47 percent) of the ND participants perceived their spouses as needing emotional or moral support, compared with the CD group (33 percent). In addition, more CD participants (54 percent) reported not being able to live up to their families' expectations, compared to 15 percent for the ND group.

The groups did not differ significantly in their immediate goals: to be healthy (34 percent), find a better or new job (30 percent), buy a house (9 percent), just be happy (9 percent), save money (8 percent), fulfill obligations to family (5 percent), visit the Philippines (4 percent), pay debts (1 percent), and others. Middle- or long-term goals included educating children and having a stable financial status (24 percent), buying a house (18 percent), just being happy (14 percent), visiting the Philippines (14 percent), paying debts (12 percent), being healthy (9 percent), getting rich or saving money (3 percent), and others (2 percent). The groups also did not differ significantly on whether they thought they could reach their goals; 90 percent thought that they could. The remaining 10 percent (mostly CD) reported

Table 3.2. Immigration and Family Profiles of Clinically Depressed and Nondepressed Filipino Americans.

Characteristics	*Clinically Depressed (CD) (n = 110)*		*Nondepressed (ND) (n = 78)*	
	Number	*Percentage*	*Number*	*Percentage*
Immigration: entry visa				
Immigrant/permanent resident/U.S. citizen	76	69.1	62	79.4
Tourist/business	23	20.6	9	11.5
Student/working	4	3.6	5	6.4
Other (e.g., fiancée)	7	6.4	2	2.7
Primary reason for coming to U.S.[a]				
To have a better life/find a job	60	57.2	30	39.5
To join spouse or family	15	14.2	28	36.8
To study/work/other	30	28.5	18	23.7
Immigration problems	13	11.8	3	3.8
Expired visa	4	3.6	0	0
Working illegally	4	3.6	2	2.5
Married to change visa	2	1.8	0	0
Other	3	2.8	1	1.3

Family: history of emotional and/or mental problems[b]				
Family history of problems with depression	41	37.3	8	10.3
Family history of alcoholism	12	10.9	5	6.4
Family history of both depression and alcoholism	25	22.7	4	5
Family history of other emotional or mental problems	3	2.7	2	1.7
Spouse's nationality[c]				
Filipino	62	72.9	48	88.9
Non-Filipino	23	27.1	6	11.1
Mean age of spouse (years, SD)	(47.4, *SD* = 16.3)		(50.1, *SD* = 15.5)	
Reason for marriage				
For love	55	75.3	43	89.6
To change visa	7	9.6	0	0
To obey parents	3	4.1	0	0
For convenience/to be able to come to U.S./other	8	11.0	5	10.4
All children also in U.S.[d]				
Yes	27	38.6	34	63
No	43	61.4	20	37
Average number of children	(3.9)		(3.5)	
Range	(1–12)		(1–10)	
Family income per year[e]				
$10,000 and below	64	58.2	24	30.8
$20,001–$35,000	23	20.9	27	34.6
35,001–$50,000	15	13.6	11	14.1
Above $50,000	8	7.3	16	20.5

[a]Significant difference between CD and ND groups ($\bar{x}^2 = 18.3$, $df = 9$, $p = 0.03$).
[b]Significant difference between CD and ND groups ($\bar{x}^2 = 14.7$, $df = 5$, $p < 0.02$).
[c]Significant difference between CD and ND groups ($p = 0.03$, Fisher's exact test, 2-tail).
[d]Significant difference between CD and ND groups ($p = 0.01$, Fisher's exact test, 2-tail).
[e]Significant difference between CD and ND groups ($\bar{x}^2 = 9.9$, $df = 1$, $p < 0.002$).

feeling hopeless, having no job, having low income, and not having enough education as common reasons for not being able to realize their goals. Of the ND group, 65 percent felt a sense of accomplishment in life; only 37 percent of the CD group had the same feeling. The main reasons cited by the CD group for not having a sense of accomplishment were inability to achieve their goals in the U.S. (24 percent), problems with marriage (21 percent), not having a preferred job (15 percent), not having fulfilled obligations to family (15 percent), problems with children (10 percent), not having finished their studies (9 percent), and others (6 percent). There were no significant differences between the two groups on means of attaining goals in the United States. The usual stated means of attaining goals in the United States included working harder (45 percent), praying to God (21 percent), finding a new or better job (16 percent), saving money (15 percent), and just waiting and/or asking for help from relatives (2 percent).

Psychosocial Stressors

Stressors of varying severity in nine categories were identified as significantly different between the CD and ND groups, both in existence and in time of occurrence (see Table 3.3). Both groups perceived multiple stressors, but the CD group perceived significantly more. The most common stressors believed to be causes of depression were geographical separation or alienation from family and financial difficulties (due to unemployment, underemployment, and low income, or financial losses). Significant psychosocial stressors that actually were correlated with clinical depression, in both occurrence and negative impact, were divorce; separation from spouse or partner due to personal conflict; parents', children's, and other family members' inability to understand or communicate with one another; decreased closeness among family members; unemployment; significant worsening of financial and social status; having no one to share leisure time with; significant decreases in sleep; and inability to have children.

Other stressors were reported more often by the CD group but showed no significant difference in impact on both groups.

Table 3.3. Existence of Perceived Significant Stressors of Clinically Depressed (CD, $n = 110$) and Nondepressed (ND, $n = 78$) Filipino Americans.

	Group	*Did Not Exist*		*Existed Within 6 Months*		*Existed Within 7 to 12 Months*	
Stressors		*N*	*%*	*N*	*%*	*N*	*%*
Family							
Geographical separation or	CD	47	43.1	23	21.1	9	8.3[a]
alienation from family	ND	52	66.7	9	11.5	4	5.1
Divorce[b]	CD	93	84.5	6	5.5	6	5.5
	ND	75	96.2	0	0	0	0
Separation from spouse due	CD	86	78.2	13	11.8	1	0.9[a]
to personal conflict[b]	ND	73	93.6	0	0	2	2.6
Current marital conflict	CD	72	65.5	22	20.0	7	6.4[a]
	ND	67	85.9	4	5.1	1	1.3
Inadequate or poor com-	CD	54	49.1	25	22.7	6	5.5[a]
munication with family	ND	54	69.2	14	17.9	2	2.6
Decrease in closeness of	CD	55	50.0	19	17.3	9	8.2[a]
family members	ND	55	70.5	10	12.8	5	6.4
Family member moving into	CD	107	97.3	2	1.8	1	0.9
participant's household	ND	69	88.5	6	7.7	2	2.6
Change in family's rank or	CD	90	81.8	7	6.4	4	3.6
status	ND	73	93.6	1	1.3		2.6
Home and Community Environment							
Change of residence[b]	CD	60	54.4	24	21.8	16	14.5
	ND	55	70.5	14	17.9	4	5.1
Search for a place to "live in"	CD	83	75.5	22	20.0	4	3.6
	ND	69	88.5	8	10.3	1	1.3
Poor living conditions[b]	CD	83	75.5	15	13.6	4	3.6[a]
	ND	71	91.0	1	1.3	4	5.1
Lack of privacy in living	CD	79	71.8	22	20.0	2	1.8
situation	ND	68	87.2	4	5.1	3	3.8
Uncomfortable sleeping area	CD	94	85.5	12	10.9	0	0
	ND	74	94.9	1	1.3	0	0
Racial discrimination in the	CD	99	90.0	5	4.5	2	1.8
community (mostly employment-related)	ND	76	97.4	0	0	1	1.3
Financial Issues							
Loss of job due to closure of firm	CD	103	93.6	4	3.6	2	1.8[a]
	ND	64	82.1	9	11.5	1	1.3
Not enough income	CD	39	35.5	37	33.6	19	17.3[a]
	ND	48	61.5	19	24.4	3	3.8

Table 3.3. Existence of Perceived Significant Stressors of Clinically Depressed (CD, $n = 110$) and Nondepressed (ND, $n = 78$) Filipino Americans, Cont'd.

	Group	*Did Not Exist*		*Existed Within 6 Months*		*Existed Within 7 to 12 Months*	
Stressors		*N*	*%*	*N*	*%*	*N*	*%*
Significant lowering of financial status	CD	48	43.6	37	33.6	16	14.5[c]
	ND	57	73.1	15	19.2	4	5.1
Borrowing (less than $10,000)	CD	94	85.5	10	9.1	3	2.7
	ND	74	94.9	3	3.8	0	0
Inability to pay bills[b]	CD	83	75.5	22	20.0	3	2.7[a]
	ND	72	92.3	3	3.8	1	1.3
Health							
Significant change in sleeping habits (much less sleep)	CD	34	30.9	59	53.6	10	9.1[c]
	ND	54	69.2	19	24.4	2	2.6
Significant change in eating habits	CD	80	72.7	17	15.5	8	4.5
Eating much more	ND	67	85.9	5	6.4	2	2.6
Eating much less	CD	57	51.8	43	39.1	8	7.3[c]
	ND	67	85.9	9	11.5	2	2.6
Being underweight	CD	92	83.6	14	12.7	2	1.8[a]
	ND	75	96.2	1	1.3	1	1.3
Taking too many drugs	CD	98	89.1	7	6.4	4	3.6
	ND	77	98.7	0	0	0	0
Work and School							
Too much pressure to achieve	CD	68	61.8	11	10.0	5	4.5[a]
	ND	64	82.1	6	7.7	2	2.6
Fear of failing or of disappointing parents	CD	83	75.5	4	4.5	1	0.9
	ND	68	87.2	3	3.8	2	2.6
Unemployment/search for a job[b]	CD	58	42.7	40	36.4	10	9.12[a]
	ND	66	84.6	10	12.8	1	1.3
Feeling of being discriminated against in school or at work	CD	91	82.7	9	8.2	3	2.7[a]
	ND	74	94.9	2	2.6	1	1.3
Personal Relationships and Social Life							
(women): Sexual difficulties of husband or male partner	CD	99	90.0	6	5.5	3	2.7
	ND	77	98.7	0	0	0	0
Lowering or loss of social status[b]	CD	45	40.9	30	27.3	8	7.3
	ND	47	60.3	9	11.5	6	7.7
Decreased social activities[b]	CD	59	53.6	29	26.4	5	4.5
	ND	55	70.5	11	14.1	3	3.8
Unassertiveness	CD	77	70.0	11	10.0	1	0.9[a]
	ND	68	87.2	4	5.1	1	1.3

Table 3.3. Existence of Perceived Significant Stressors of Clinically Depressed (CD, $n = 110$) and Nondepressed (ND, $n = 78$) Filipino Americans, Cont'd.

	Group	*Did Not Exist*		*Existed Within 6 Months*		*Existed Within 7 to 12 Months*	
Stressors		*N*	*%*	*N*	*%*	*N*	*%*
Difficulty communicating with children and/or parents	CD	68	87.2	13	11.8	6	5.5
	ND	64	82.1	6	7.7	3	3.8
Feeling of loneliness, alienation[b]	CD	26	23.6	56	50.9	10	9.1[c]
	ND	53	67.9	13	16.7	6	7.7
Feeling of rejection, abandonment[b]	CD	58	52.7	36	32.7	4	3.6[c]
	ND	69	88.5	5	6.4	1	1.3
Inability to form and/or maintain friendships[b]	CD	97	88.2	4	3.6	1	0.9
	ND	76	97.4	1	1.3	0	0
Feeling of being different from other people[b]	CD	74	67.3	14	12.7	5	4.5[a]
	ND	67	85.9	2	2.6	0	0
Adjustment to American life	CD	62	46.4	15	13.6	9	8.2
	ND	56	71.8	9	11.5	5	6.4
Leisure/Recreation/Religion							
Not enough resources to do what participant enjoys[b]	CD	59	53.9	30	27.3	10	9.1[a]
	ND	60	76.9	10	12.8	3	3.8
Loss of interest in usual things and/or recreational activities[b]	CD	68	61.8	27	24.5	6	5.5[c]
	ND	75	96.2	3	3.8	0	0
Too much time on hands	CD	91	82.7	10	9.1	2	1.8
	ND	74	94.9	3	3.8	1	1.3
Lack of people to share leisure time with	CD	81	73.6	17	15.5	4	3.6[c]
	ND	75	96.2	2	2.6	1	1.3
Inability to do the things the participant enjoys, due to physical or mental disabilities[b]	CD	82	74.5	20	18.2	3	2.7
	ND	69	88.5	3	3.8	4	5.1
Legal Problems							
Immigration problems	CD	92	83.6	7	6.4	5	4.5
	ND	73	93.6	2	2.6	1	1.3
Court hearings[b]	CD	96	87.3	10	9.1	2	1.8
	ND	75	96.2	2	2.6	0	0
Verbal abuse (usually by spouse)	CD	94	85.5	7	6.4	3	2.7
	ND	74	94.9	1	1.3	1	1.3
Having something stolen from home	CD	99	90.0	5	4.5	2	1.8
	ND	76	97.4	1	1.3	0	0
Mental/Emotional Problems							
Feelings of worthlessness[b]	CD	62	56.4	37	33.6	5	4.5[c]
	ND	71	91.0	3	3.8	2	2.6
Feelings of hopelessness[b]	CD	70	63.6	30	27.3	4	3.6[c]
	ND	74	97.9	2	2.6	2	2.6

Table 3.3. Existence of Perceived Significant Stressors of Clinically Depressed (CD, $n = 110$) and Nondepressed (ND, $n = 78$) Filipino Americans, Cont'd.

	Group	Did Not Exist		Existed Within 6 Months		Existed Within 7 to 12 Months	
Stressors		*N*	%	*N*	%	*N*	%
Feeling lack of personal power and control	CD	43	39.1	39	35.5	8	7.3[c]
	ND	60	76.9	10	12.8	0	0
Anxiety about health	CD	17	15.5	75	68.2	7	6.4[c]
	ND	39	50.0	31	39.7	3	3.8
Confusion[b]	CD	77	70.0	26	23.6	2	1.8[c]
	ND	73	93.6	3	3.8	1	1.3
Irritability, quickness to anger	CD	33	30.0	61	55.5	7	6.4[c]
	ND	49	62.8	24	30.8	1	1.3
Apathy[b]	CD	80	72.7	26	23.6	0	0[c]
	ND	76	97.4	1	1.3	0	0
Lack of energy for usual activities	CD	37	33.6	62	56.4	7	6.4
	ND	50	64.1	22	28.2	2	2.6

[a]$p < 0.01$

[b]Stressors significantly correlated with major depression (severe, with and without psychotic features; Spearman rho, value = 0.19, $t = 2.3$, $p \lessapprox 0.05$).

[c]$p < 0.001$.

There were also stressors that showed significant difference in negative impact alone but similar occurrence in both groups. The CD group perceived these stressors as having more negative ("bad") effects on them, compared to what was perceived by nondepressed group. These psychosocial stressors included recent serious illness or injury in the family, physical or emotional separation from family, marital conflict, recent marriage, problems with in-laws, inability to save money, personal medical problems, breakup with a significant other, unfaithfulness of a husband or male lover, conflict with a significant other, feeling lonely and abandoned, feeling discriminated against in work or at school, adjustment and immigration problems, feeling obligated to take care of parents, feeling tired while doing usual activities, and not having enough resources. Lack of privacy was considered the most common housing problem, but there was no statistically significant difference on this factor between the two groups. The CD group did report the highest number of persons in one household, however. There was also no significant difference between the two groups on visa and immigration status, but those who had expired visas (2 percent), who were working illegally (6 percent), and who had married to change their visa status (2 percent) had a higher rate (85 percent) of major depression than did those with no immigration problems. The "victims" or spouses of those participants who had married to change their visa status were also at high risk for clinical depression. We also observed that CD participants had experienced multiple stressors, both acute and chronic, within the preceding six months to one year. Some symptoms of depression, such as changes in sleeping and eating patterns, were also considered stressors in themselves.

Coping Resources and Responses

One perceived environmental resource that was significantly different between the groups was having someone to share problems with. Of the ND group, 87 percent had someone, but only 42 percent of the CD group did. Another significant difference was that 69 percent of the CD participants did not live with their spouses, but 50 percent of the ND group did. Some spouses in both groups were either in the Philippines or working in another place. Some couples were legally separated or divorced. In some families, the parents continued to live together even after they had divorced or legally separated, "for the sake of the children" or for financial and immigration-related reasons. Moreover, 57 percent of the CD participants did not want to share their problems with their families; 71 percent of ND group did. Reasons for not sharing problems with families included alienation, separation, denial, and language problems. No significant differences existed between the groups in terms of the persons they share their problems with: spouses and mates, partners, parents, siblings, children, religious and/or community groups, and family physicians. Religious or community groups were as likely as parents to become confidants; therefore, these resources need to be identified in planning for the prevention and treatment of depression among Filipino Americans.

Asked whether family members provided enough emotional support, the groups gave similar responses: 55 percent did not perceive enough emotional support from family members. However, the CD participants differed significantly in their perceived reasons for the failure of the family members to give enough emotional support: "they are too busy," "they're sickly," "they're far away," "they don't care," and "they have no time."

Of the ND group, 62 percent asked for help with emotional problems; only 45 percent of the CD group did. No significant difference between the groups was found in the persons they asked for help, who included family members (mostly spouses), family doctors, priest and/or religious group members, psychiatrists, and counselor and psychologists.

The CD group used the American mental health system minimally: 68 percent had never used it, but many "overused" medical and family outpatient clinics for vegetative manifestations of depression and for somatic pains (only 55 percent of all the participants were aware of existing mental health resources in their communities. Reasons given by CD participants for not using these resources included "no reason," "don't know anybody in the center," "ashamed to use it," "afraid to have mental records" that might jeopardize a job or the search for a better job, "feeling discriminated against," "center inaccessible or too far away."

Common coping strategies reported by both groups were consulting a family member, friend, or family physician (only 0.9 percent of the CD group consulted psychiatrists), engaging in religious and social activities, eating more, sleeping more, sleeping less, eating less, drinking alcoholic beverages, doing nothing, waiting and seeing, gambling, taking medications, and simply accepting things. The majority (77 percent) of all the participants believed that God would help them, but 92 percent of the CD group believed in "leaving it up to God" (only 20 percent of the ND group had this attitude).

Beliefs and Concepts

The CD participants' perceived causes of depression are listed in Table 3.4. More than 60 percent of the group reported financial

Table 3.4. Perceived Causes of Depression.

Perceived Cause	*Percentage Reporting*
Financial difficulties, underemployment or unemployment, and job-related problems	34
Said by respondent to be unknown	12
Geographical separation or alienation from loved ones	27
Strong sense of obligation; inability to fulfill obligations to family members and significant others	8
Medical problems	8
Inability to live up to expectations of parents, family members, or other loved ones	4
Retirement, death in the family, "God's punishment," and other causes	7

difficulties, unemployment or underemployment, job-related problems, and separation or alienation from loved ones as primary causes of their depression, and 12 percent did not know of any possible causes. Table 3.5 shows CD participants' beliefs regarding the best treatment for depression. Only 16 percent considered drugs to be best; 21 percent preferred counseling or psychotherapy. The majority (63 percent) did not consider medication and psychotherapy to be the best treatments; 50 percent of the CD group preferred talking with a loved one or concerned other, and the rest of the CD group mentioned a variety of other treatments or sources of relief.

Table 3.5. Beliefs About Best Treatment for Clinical Depression.

Treatment	*Percentage Reporting*
Talking with a loved one or someone else who cares	50
Counseling; psychotherapy (including group therapy)	21
Medications	16
Social and religious activities (parties, shopping; prayer groups, attending church)	10
Faith healing, finding a job, using marijuana, other treatments	3

Table 3.6. Beliefs About Best Person to Treat Clinical Depression.

Person(s)	*Percentage Reporting*
A loved one or close family member or friend	60
Family physician	15
Psychiatrist or psychologist	12
Counselor or social worker	5
Priest, faith healer, or other religious person; God	8
Others (co-worker; prayer group)	10

Note: Some participants gave multiple answers.

Table 3.6 shows CD participants' beliefs regarding the best person to treat or relieve clinical depression. Most (60 percent) mentioned a family member or close friend. It was interesting to note that, in the past, 27 percent of all the participants had consulted a priest for their problems while being treated by professionals. When the CD participants were asked what had prompted them to see a physician, 54 percent of them said that they had sought help for inability to sleep or problems with sleeping, and 21 percent had consulted physicians for muscle weakness, fatigue, dizziness, chest pains, headaches, upset stomach, and inability to think or concentrate. Only 25 percent had consulted physicians for depression.

Personality Traits and Separation History

Some personality and cultural traits that were significantly correlated with major depression and with the nondepressed group are listed in Table 3.7. The most common traits associated with clinical depression were easily hurt feelings, hypersensitivity, breaking down under stress, the tendency to worry most of the time, feeling insecure, aggression, dependence, and easily giving up or withdrawing. The ND participants had some traits in common. They were flexible, easily adjusted to others and to situations, were happy, enthusiastic, and self-confident, and had a sense of humor.

As shown by previous studies (Muñoz, 1987), children are at risk for depression later in life when separated from a primary caregiver before the age of sixteen. There was no significant difference between the two groups on history of separation from the primary caregiver during childhood, but there was

Table 3.7. Personality and Cultural Traits Correlated with Clinically Depressed and Nondepressed Filipino Americans.

	Kendall's Tau Correlation Coefficients	*p-value*
Clinically Depressed		
Easily breaking down under stress	.41	.0001
Feeling insecure	.43	.0001
Easily hurt feelings	.47	.0001
Easily giving up or withdrawing	.43	.0001
Hypersensitivity	.42	.0001
Tendency to worry most of the time	.42	.0001
Belief in optimistic fatalism—inevitability of one's faith	.23	not significant
Dependence	.19	not significant
Aggression	.29	.006
Normal		
Flexible	.295	.004
Easily adjusted to others	.274	.007
Easily found ways to solve problems	.234	not significant
Ambitious	.194	not significant
Intelligent	.196	not significant
Tolerant	.28	.007
Self-confident	.267	.009
Easily adjusted to situation	.295	.004
Sense of humor	.27	.008
Happy	.398	.0002
Courageous	.247	.016
Enthusiastic	.38	.0002

a significant difference in duration of such separation. The CD participants had experienced longer separations than the ND group. The usual causes for separation were sequential emigration (one or both parents had emigrated ahead of the children, or vice versa), demands of work, and illness or death.

Conclusions

The demographic findings with regard to clinically depressed participants in this study are consistent with previous studies reporting that low-income, less educated, and unemployed or underemployed people are more likely to become depressed (Muñoz, 1988; Liem and Liem, 1978; Kessler, 1979). The social-causation or social-selection hypothesis asserts that those of lower socioeconomic status experience more environmental stressors, such as financial difficulties and poor health (Liem and Liem, 1978) and are more vulnerable to the ill effects of various stressors. This susceptibility may be due both to less effective coping strategies and to inadequate personal and community resources (Kessler, 1979). In this study, there was no significant difference on gender between the clinically depressed and nondepressed groups, which implies that Filipino American men and women are equally at risk for depression.

Participants' beliefs regarding causes, best treatments, and best persons to treat clinical depression reflect the participants' overall understanding of this affective disorder. When they perceived financial difficulties, unemployment, and separation and alienation from loved ones as causes of depression, they tended not to complain about these problems to physicians or psychiatrists, who might not be perceived as able to help. Such beliefs may also explain why more than 60 percent of our clinically depressed participants preferred to use their own social support systems rather than consult mental health professionals for depression, yet they did consult physicians for somatic and vegetative symptoms.

Of the significant psychosocial stressors found to be correlated with clinical depression, more than 60 percent are considered severe (divorce, unemployment) or moderate (marital conflicts, separation) and either acute (physical illness) or enduring (poverty or financial difficulties). Divorce among Filipino Americans should perhaps be considered not severe but catastrophic, as we have seen.

The clinically depressed participants had significantly more stressors than the nondepressed group. This circumstance can be expected to have cumulative effects on emotional, mental, and physical well-being and on personal resources. Moreover, one severe and enduring stressor, such as unemployment, can produce additional stressors, such as frequent marital conflict, communication and interpersonal problems, and physical and psychiatric illness. In addition, stress erodes feelings of social competence and self-esteem; when "nothing seems to work out," learned helplessness (Seligman, 1975) may become an issue and a stressor in itself.

The negative impacts of various stressors (especially immigration-related problems) were perceived as more intense among the clinically depressed participants than among the nondepressed group. This finding seems to support Beck's cognitive theory of depression: that depressed individuals have a "distorted structuring of perceptual experiences," which results in negative perceptions of their environment and of themselves (Beck, 1967). But it is equally true that the effects of psychosocial stressors may be effectively buffered by personal and environment resources (Billings and Moos, 1982), such as having someone to share problems with or being a member of an ethnic or religious organization. Certain premorbid personality and cultural traits may precipitate or aggravate depression, but an attitude of optimistic fatalism—"it's up to God"—may also serve as a coping mechanism to help Filipino Americans accept some of the stressors that are beyond their control.

Feelings of insecurity or inferiority may have reflected low self-esteem among the clinically depressed group, while the nondepressed group reported more self-confidence. A sense of mastery over the environment, together with adequate self-esteem, can buffer the depressive effects of psychosocial stressors (Pearlin and Schooler, 1978). One of the most important social-environmental resources is the availability of supportive individuals, such as close family members, loved ones, friends, and religious counselors. Having a confidant or someone to share problems with has a stress-buffering effect; having no one seems to increase vulnerability to depression.

The full effects of immigration on the participants in this study were not assessed, but some of the effects are suggested by the significant difference found between the nondepressed and depressed groups on length of separation from the primary caregiver (and from other family members).

Genetic or biological determinants associated with depression were highly supported by this study, with a significant positive family history of clinical depression among the depressed group. Specific Filipino American beliefs, as well as personality and culture traits, may also increase or decrease susceptibility to clinical depression.

Chapter 4

Schizophrenia, Acute Psychoses, Culture-Bound Syndromes, and Other Mental Disorders

The medical literature has recorded how different cultural settings, different times, and different circumstances in history have colored the presentation of many mental disorders. For example, posttraumatic stress disorder was delineated by war conditions. Hysteria was much written about in Freud's time. Anorexia nervosa is predominant in the United States and other industrialized countries, but not so in Third World countries. Suicide is more prevalent in some cultures than in others. Paranoid disorder has been recognized as a special problem among immigrants in general and refugees in particular (Westermeyer, 1993). Somatization has been noted as an Asian inclination in symptom formation (Kuo, 1984).

This chapter examines how Filipino culture and the Filipino American immigration experience have influenced the presentation of some mental conditions. Schizophrenic disorder, the acute psychoses, panic disorder, adjustment disorder, and culture-bound syndromes are discussed in terms of prominent Filipino American sociocultural influences.

Schizophrenic Disorders

The schizophrenic disorders are a distinct group of serious psychotic conditions whose incidence seems to vary little worldwide. All races are affected, and the personality deterioration and insidious cost of schizophrenia cause a downward drift in the afflicted person's socioeconomic status. Because of their chronicity, high degree of recurrence, and early onset, the schizophrenic disorders account for a large number of admissions to psychiatric wards, sometimes estimated to be 25 percent of first admissions to U.S. public mental institutions.

No systematic nationwide study has been conducted on the prevalence of the schizophrenic disorders among Filipino Americans in this country or among native Filipinos. There are indications, however, that among Filipino American patients in U.S. psychiatric hospitals and clinics, this diagnosis is highly represented and therefore deserves closer scrutiny (see Figures 4.1 and 4.2).

In the Philippines

In the Philippines, schizophrenic disorders are a major mental health problem, the result of many distinct factors. At the National Center for Mental Health, in Mandaluyong, Metro Manila, schizophrenic disorders comprised over 70 percent of all inpatient admissions between January and December of 1989. During the same months, schizophrenic disorders accounted for 43.8 percent of all charitable outpatient consultations at the same center (see Figures 4.3 and 4.4).

Schizophrenic disorders were also highly represented in Dr. Sustento-Seneriches's private psychiatric practice in Iloilo, the Philippines, between 1977 and 1981 (Sustento-Seneriches, 1981). They comprised 70 percent of inpatient and 30 percent of outpatient cases. In the rural areas, she saw chronically schizophrenic people languishing in small bolted palm-thatched huts or stalls in backyards. At times they were tied to posts, fed through small holes, and periodically hosed down. One schizo-

Figure 4.1. Diagnostic Categories of Filipino American Outpatients at the Asian Community Mental Health Center, Oakland, California (1990–1991).

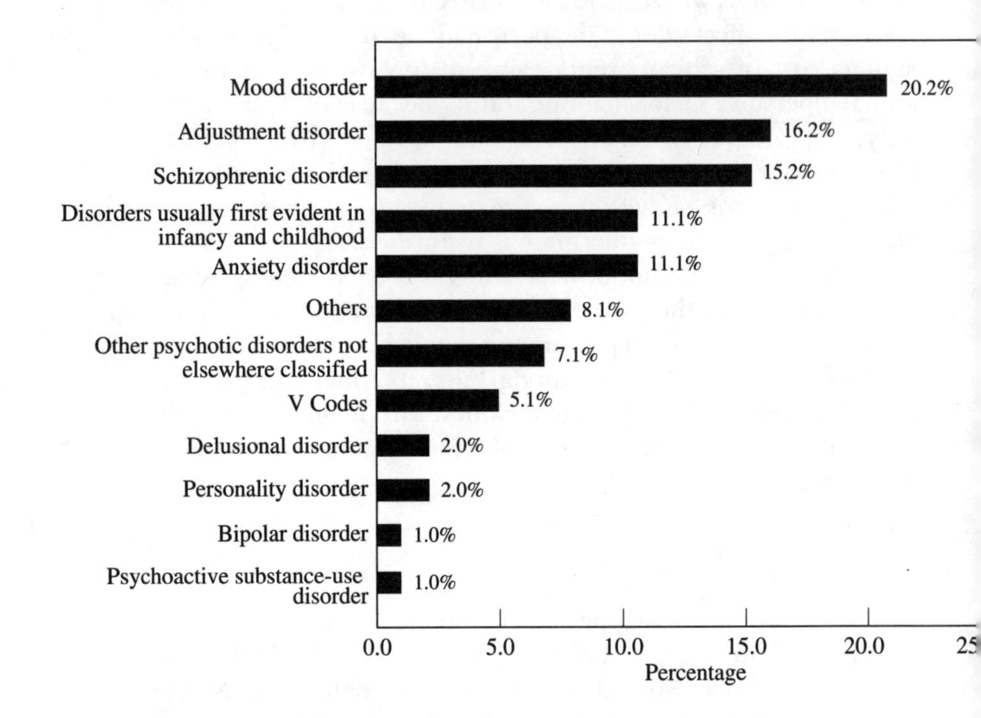

phrenic patient developed tetanus from rope wounds caused by the same rope that the family used to tie its water buffalo.

At the Asilo de Molo, in Iloilo City, a Catholic institution for orphans and the elderly, the nuns took in vagrant psychotic women. The women were put in barred cells, humanely clothed, fed, given shelter, and kept clean. Many manifested the old diagnostic entity of hebephrenic schizophrenia. All were recurrently and chronically schizophrenic. A program implemented by the new medical school, the city health department, and the local Soroptimist Club eventually gave free psychiatric treatment and follow-up to this unfortunate group. Still, medications were not consistently available.

Figure 4.2. Diagnostic Categories of Filipino American Inpatients at San Francisco General Hospital, Psychiatry Ward 7-C (1982–1984).

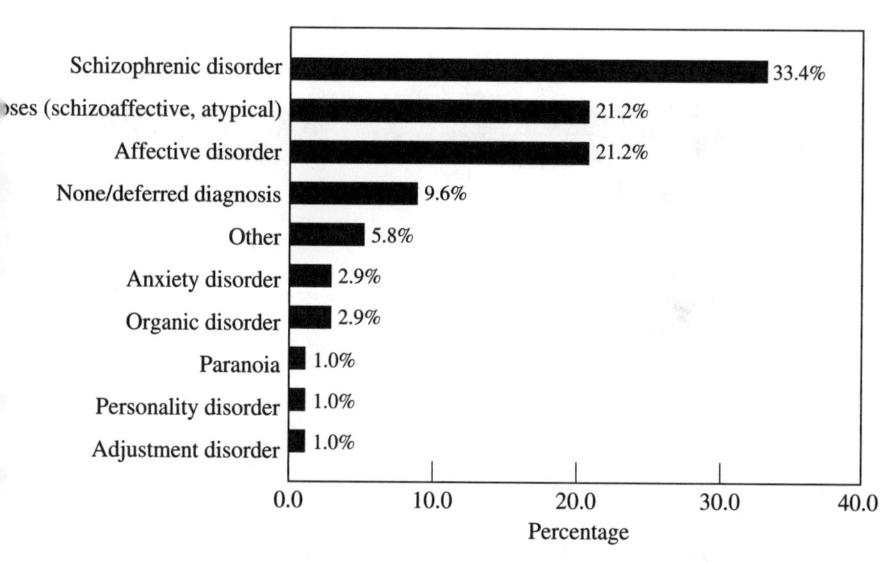

In the United States

The foremost factors in the Philippines—poor economic conditions, and therefore lack of access to consistent medication and other treatments—are not present to such a dramatic and overwhelming extent in the United States. There are, however, persistent hindrances to the early detection and treatment of these disorders in the Filipino American community. Indeed, schizophrenic disorders account for a significant number of Filipino American patients' diagnoses when treatment is finally sought (see again Figures 4.1 and 4.2).

Cultural Hindrances to Early Treatment

Because the course of schizophrenia is generally unabated despite well-meaning concern, familial caretaking, and friendly advice, the Filipino American schizophrenic patient eventually does end up seeking help or being brought to a helping agency.

Figure 4.3. Diagnostic Categories of Inpatients at the National Center for Mental Health, Mandaluyong, Manila (January–December 1989).

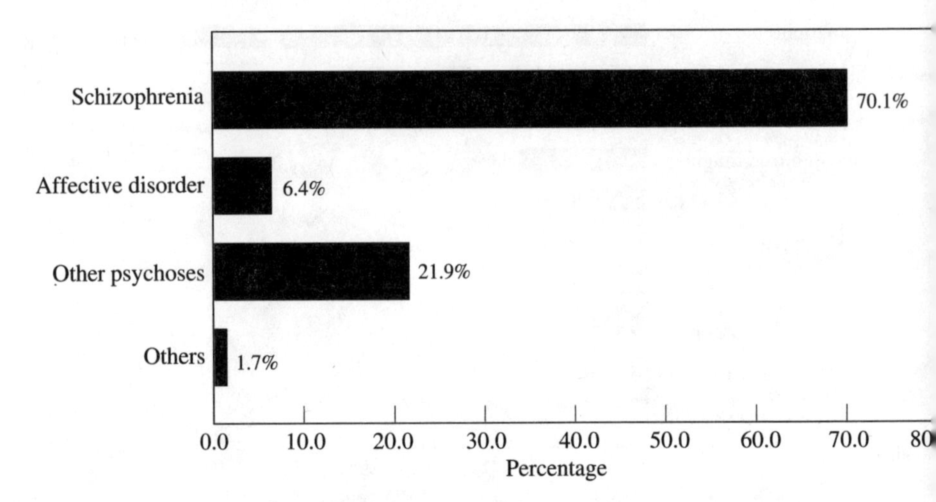

Vignette. *A thirty-two-year-old single unemployed engineer joined his sister's family and his widowed mother in the San Francisco Bay area. His mother sponsored his entry into the United States directly from the Philippines. The family members considered him the most intelligent of all the siblings and accepted and tolerated him as an eccentric bachelor. They gave him aspirin for his headaches, attributing them to his constant reading.*

He began having problems holding a job. He also began to keep to himself, staying in his room and many times eating his meals there as well. Sometimes he would tell his mother about the convictions that God had relayed directly to him.

Two years later, when he started exposing himself to neighbors, his family brought him to a psychiatrist, recommended by a friend who was a Filipino American internist. It was no coincidence that the psychiatrist was a considerable distance away from the family's predominantly Filipino American community.

Figure 4.4. Diagnostic Categories of Outpatients at the National Center for Mental Health, Mandaluyong, Manila (January–December 1989).

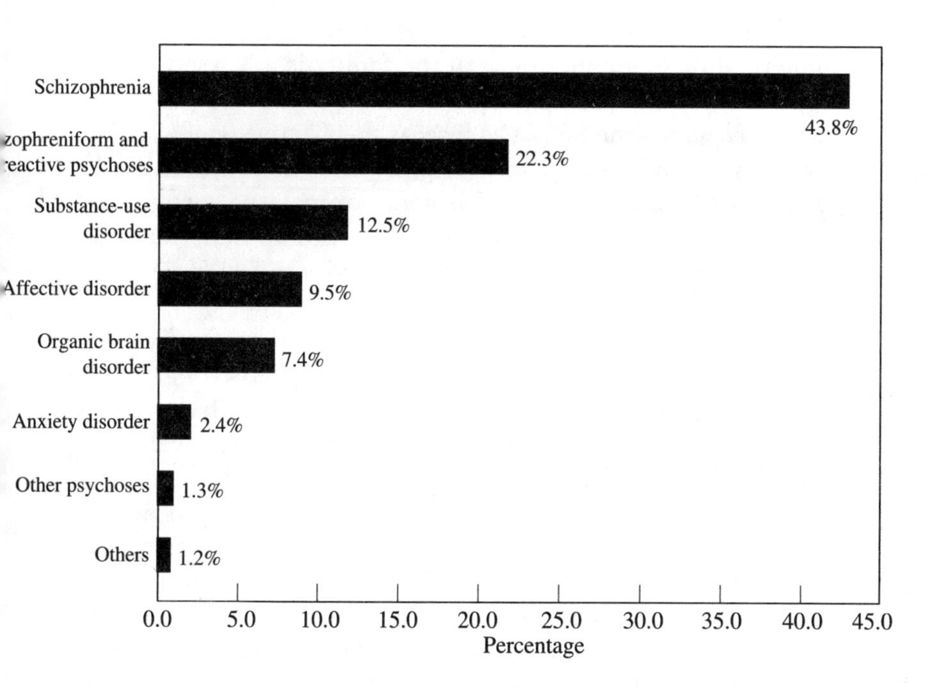

What cultural factors deter patients and their families from seeking help earlier? First, there is the big factor of stigma. Acknowledging mental illness, even by seeking help, is acknowledging the presence of "bad blood" and weakness in the entire family or clan. This is true also in other Asian American groups, where the goal of preserving family integrity inhibits the seeking of proper treatment (Sue and Morishima, 1982). When individual identity is closely attached to the clan's identity, this factor is understandable.

We suspect that this factor is emphasized in the Philippines because of the archipelago itself. Bodies of water, poor transportation, and poorer finances separate many of the seven thousand islands and their inhabitants. This separation encourages a sense of regionalism, which may have been brought in (if not promoted) by the Spaniards with their divide-and-conquer policy during their three-century rule of the Philippines (Del

Rosario, 1990). In the Philippine archipelago, the presence of psychotic illness among the members of a clan living in a small town or on an island can indeed be visible and may be a source of considerable social embarrassment and stigma. The marriage potential of single members of the family is adversely affected by the known presence of psychosis in the family.

Hiya, shame or loss of face, is an effective way of curtailing unwanted behavior in the family and the community. Using *hiya* to discipline a child is common paternal or authority behavior in the Philippine culture (Sustento-Seneriches and Ladrido-Ignacio, 1983), and the proclivity to feel *hiya* is a predominant personality trait.

There is the factor of the Filipino American family's tolerance of regressive behavior in its members. A strong cultural expectation is for the family to take care of its elderly, young, and sick or weak members. Patience, tolerance, loyalty, and even suffering in the process of caring for these dependent members are seen by the Filipino American community as admirable qualities. Unfortunately, this tendency can cause patients and their families to seek help only when symptoms are severely disruptive of family and community life. When the behavior becomes threatening to the patient's well-being (as when the catatonic patient does not eat for days), or when the behavior threatens family integrity (as when the patient is violent or becomes a source of embarrassment), the family is mobilized to curtail the behavior and ask for help.

Another compelling factor is Filipinos' general unfamiliarity with psychiatry as a medical discipline, as well as their strong familiarity with age-old indigenous explanations of and ministrations for emotional problems (Sustento-Seneriches, 1984). In the Philippines, it is not uncommon to observe the schizophrenic process in its full chronicity and regression, without the intervention of psychotropics (although this phenomenon is more common in the rural hinterlands than in the affluent cities). In Dr. Sustento-Seneriches's current psychiatric practice, in Pleasanton, California, there is observably less chronicity among Filipino American schizophrenic patients than among those who were in her Philippine practice. Nevertheless, the family's tendency not to seek help early persists.

Still another factor is the population's observed lack of familiarity with the American medical system and lack of confidence in the relevance of psychiatry to emotional distress. Filipino psychiatric patients have more confidence in the help of their families, their churches, their family doctors, and even their children's pediatricians than in the help available from mental health clinics. Even in the United States, they still seek the advice of their priests for exorcism, their saints for healing intercessions, their traditional healers for rituals, incantations, and herbs, and their God-chosen healers who go into religious trances. There are also those (especially Filipinos of Chinese ancestry) who seek the advice of seers.

> **Vignette.** *A female college freshman, the youngest of three children of professional Filipino American immigrants, was admitted in a mute, staring, catatonic state to the psychiatric unit. Facing some difficulties in her academic studies and her college social life, she had begun losing sleep. An initial preoccupation with a male classmate progressed to frank persecutory delusions. These included delusions of being courted by fairies from the nearby park. Frightened, she locked all the windows and doors and performed ritualistic calesthenics before she became mute and catatonic.*
>
> *Her parents and her A-student sisters had realized that the family's and the patient's dream of being a scientist might be out of her reach. They had tried to soothe her, had taken time from their own work and studies to stay up late with her, and had made sure that she ate properly. It was only when she became catatonic and rigid and seemed to stop breathing that they feared for her life and took her to the emergency room.*
>
> *She was hospitalized for a month, and for the next three years she had almost yearly acute recurrences. Unable to return to college, she remained an eccentric loner. Her family history included a schizophrenic disorder in a maternal aunt and a grandfather.*

There are groups of symptoms and clinical presentations commonly agreed to justify a diagnosis of schizophrenia, but distinctive cultural influences can produce variances in many ways. Characteristic symptoms are delusions, hallucinations, catatonic behavior, inappropriate affect, and disturbances of functioning in many areas of life (self-care, work, interpersonal relating), which manifestations are not due to any organic cause. The schizophrenic process runs for at least six months, with at least one week in the active phase, when the disruption is full-blown. There may also be a preceding prodromal phase, with early signs of deterioration, and a long-drawn-out residual phase after the active phase.

Commonly observed delusions and hallucinations among Filipino American patients are those that concern religion (Enwright and Jaeckle, 1962), sex, threatening authority figures (Sechrest, 1969), and powerful external forces (radar, planets). In their psychotic systems, very recent immigrants or unacculturated Filipinos may bring in the supernatural world of witches, fairies, benevolent or malevolent dwarfs living in termite hills, beings from the sea or the forests, giants, and souls (Tan, 1987). Recent sociopolitical and environmental events in the Philippines ("people power," the revolution of 1986, the Mount Pinatubo eruption) may also be incorporated into symptomatology.

Dr. Sustento-Seneriches has observed a tendency among Filipino American patients in general to be freer and more dramatic in showing emotions than are unacculturated Japanese patients. This observation is in contrast to the generalized notion that Asian patients are subdued and restrained (Sue and Morishima, 1982; Leong, 1986).

Implications

There is a compelling need for psychoeducation in the Filipino American community on the early signs of schizophrenic disorders, the efficacy of psychiatric treatment, and the need for early treatment to prevent further deterioration and complications. Mental health clinics should devise culturally relevant treatments and outreach programs for their Filipino American clientele.

When schizophrenic patients are brought over to this country by their families, the stress of the immigration experience can provoke an acute episode. The factors of chronicity and inconsistent medication in the Philippines, with complications like tardive dyskinesia, should be borne in mind. Phenothiazines, specifically Thorazine (chlorpromazine), are the most common psychotropic drugs used in the Philippines.

Acute Psychoses

This group of psychoses among Filipino American clientele deserves special discussion. The acute psychoses, as they are called in the literature, are found and documented more frequently in developing countries than in developed countries. Therefore, clinicians trained and experienced in the United States may not be familiar with the cultural presentations of these psychoses and may misdiagnose them, preventing a better prognosis than schizophrenic disorder, and preventing the use of specific culturally relevant treatments.

Shon (1972), in his study of fifty-one immigrants admitted to the University of California at San Francisco's Langley Porter Neuropsychiatric Institute between 1968 and 1972, observes that 43 percent of the Philippine-born patients were diagnosed mainly as schizophrenics. He wonders whether these patients were all truly schizophrenics, or whether they were suffering instead from an adjustment reaction. They might have been more accurately diagnosed as acutely psychotic. Moreover, "in most cases, a precipitating event involving loss of self-esteem was present, e.g., failing a licensure exam, a professional unable to obtain a position in her field and forced to take a menial job, or a wife discovering her husband was dating other women" (p. 16).

Differential Diagnosis

As in the schizophrenic and bipolar disorders, there is no organic factor that initiates and maintains the disturbance. By contrast with the schizophrenic and bipolar disorders, there is not likely to be a history of schizophrenia or bipolar disorder among first-degree relatives. Also by contrast with the schizophrenic disorders, there is no chronic deterioration of the patient's personality, and the prognosis is definitely better. And, by contrast with the bipolar-disordered patient, the acutely psychotic patient's excitability is without the exuberant affect.

Clinical Presentations

Acute psychosis features a very rapid onset, an identifiable precipitating stressor, a variable florid psychotic presentation (often with a predominantly different clinical feel in comparison to the recognized form of schizophrenic or affective illness), and a relatively short course of symptomatology (often with a tendency for the patient to clear with or without treatment).

> **Vignette.** *A Filipino American woman of Chinese ancestry was referred by her parish priest. She was preoccupied and agitated about her and her husband's new apartment. According to Chinese folk beliefs, the front door and the windows were not correctly situated in relation to the sun, and this forebode misfortune for the family. She aimlessly ran around the house, disoriented at times. She began having suspicions and ideas of reference (a sudden storm, earthquake predictions in the news that she thought were related to her, in a fashion still unclear). Although described by her husband and her brother as sensitive and superstitious in the past, she had never experienced an incident similar to this one. There was also no family history of major psychiatric illness.*
>
> *The symptoms had begun when she received a letter from her mother in the Philippines, chiding her for not helping out in the construction of "the family house" in the Philippines. The patient's husband had also just lost some money gambling in Reno.*
>
> *The patient was initially diagnosed by the emergency-room doctor as schizophrenic, and she*

> *was promptly given Haloperidol to tone down her marked agitation. The extrapyramidal side effects frightened her, worsening the paranoid ideation and agitation. With small amounts of Mellaril (thioridazine) and intensive use of marital and individual psychotherapies, her condition abated within two weeks.*

One distinctive symptom may be confusion. Patients may wander aimlessly, and be unable to say why. They may also appear puzzled and bewildered and be unable to recognize family members or be in touch with their immediate surroundings. Auditory hallucinations may be common, as well as delusions of control, reference, and persecution. Psychomotor excitement is often the reason why help is sought. Restlessness, throwing things around, sexual disinhibition, shouting, and singing were often observed in those with schizophrenic psychosis and in those diagnosed as having some other, nonorganic psychosis in Ladrido-Ignacio's study at the Philippine Mental Hospital (1985). There may also be a flair for drama or histrionic, attention-seeking behavior. Other observed symptoms may be stupor, mutism, and hypomanic affect. There may be paranoid, passive, schizoid, explosive, or histrionic personality patterns.

Dr. Sustento-Seneriches has observed several precipitating stressors among Filipino American patients: family and marital conflicts, extramarital affairs, embarrassment and inadequacies in work situations (including perceived discrimination), estrangement from the Philippine family, jet lag on the initial immigration journey, financial problems, and accidents or illness.

Implications

As implied by the foregoing discussion, the clinician can expect to find this group of psychoses among unacculturated Filipino Americans and recent Filipino immigrants. Those coming from rural areas, or from the lower socioeconomic urban populace in the Philippines, will manifest more regressive features.

Panic Disorder

In addition to intense subjective fear, the symptoms of panic disorder are physiological (that is, they entail hyperstimulation of the autonomic nervous system). It is in the interpretation of these physical symptoms that distinctly cultural factors play a big role among Filipino American patients.

> **Vignette.** *A highly successful Filipino American woman professional experienced cold clammy perspiration, rapid heartbeat, difficulty in breathing, and a terrible conviction of impending doom. She was rushed from work to the hospital's emergency room. Told that her heart was normal, she went home and promptly had another attack that night. She sought one cardiologist's opinion and then another's, becoming increasingly panicked. She carried hot-water bottles to prevent the cold clammy feelings, and she dressed warmly to avoid drafts. She also went on vacation, slowed her physical exertions, said the rosary every night and became involved with Catholic devotional prayer groups in her area.*

Cultural Explanations

The presence of hot flushes and cold, sweaty extremities readily invokes *pasma,* a widespread explanation of illness causation found mainly among Christian Filipino groups. *Pasma* involves beliefs about the interaction between hot and cold, the state of health being a balance of both (Tan, 1987). When they feel cold clammy perspiration, it is not unusual for panicked Filipino American patients who believe in *pasma* to reach repeatedly for drinks of hot water, which they carry with them in anticipation of the next attack. They may wear warm clothing or carry wool blankets in which to bundle up, even during psychiatric interviews. Then, when they experience hot flushing, they may desperately rush out into cool air or open windows to let cool air in.

Folk perceptions of anatomy and physiology can dictate cultural reactions to physical symptoms. One common Filipino explanation for illness involves perspiration drying on the skin; a nervously perspiring Filipino American who believes in this explanation may wrap up to avoid "dangerous" drafts.

Muscular pain from anxiety states may be interpreted as bodily sensitivity to "hot" or "cold." The back is especially sensitive to drafts (Tan, 1987). The legs, arms, feet, and hands are meticulously kept away from cold water after an episode of such "hot" activity as typing, writing, running, or prolonged standing. To prevent muscular pain, patients may not wash after such activities. Their heads must likewise be protected from drafts and evening dew, to prevent headaches.

The heart, the blood, the brain, the liver, and the gall bladder are vital organs in Filipino folk concepts of anatomy and physiology (Tan, 1987). Even traditional healers readily take the pulse as a diagnostic tool. Irregularities of the pulse, and rapid pounding of the heart or audible heart activity, may readily become the sensitizing focus of panic-disordered patients, who become deathly afraid that they have fatal heart conditions or are having "strokes." Hyperventilation and hypoventilation may be related to "heart attacks" as well.

These patients may seek help from a family physician by asking for a cure for heart disease. They may ask for iron prescriptions for "thin blood" (anemia), which they believe causes insomnia or sleep disturbances. Gastrointestinal distress is common in anxiety states and can readily be attributed to fatal conditions of the liver or gall bladder. Gas pains can be attributed to exposure to "wind," and patients may use abdominal binders to prevent these pains. In Isabela, in the northern Philippines, there exists *matalinan,* a folk illness in which intestinal colic supposedly causes stiff veins to appear on the abdomen. The patient who believes in this illness will go to a *hilot* (masseur) for massage of the knotted veins. Genitourinary symptoms can be explained by the presence of a "displaced organ" (the uterus, for example), which should then be massaged back to its proper place (Tan, 1987).

In addition to these beliefs among Christian Filipino Americans, magical explanations for anxiety symptoms may also be invoked, especially by people from the rural Philippines. Ghosts or dead spirits who are displeased or who are longing for the living (the patient) are said to cause symptoms like cold clammy extremities and belching. There may be an unexplainable cold feeling due to dead spirits, and insomnia or headaches may be attributed to the souls of children in limbo (Tan, 1987).

Sorcery and witchcraft may be invoked in the causation of anxiety symptoms and represent widespread beliefs throughout the archipelago, particularly in the non-Westernized, unsophisticated populace. In Marinduque, for example, voodoo-type sorcerers may use dolls to inflict pain on their victims.

Implications

Because of the varied cultural interpretations of somatic symptoms in panic attacks, Filipino American patients will most probably seek out family doctors before psychiatrists. Prolonged and expensive diagnostic procedures, a focus on the patient's body as the trigger of the panic, and complications like depression and phobia can be prevented by early diagnosis. The family physician who is aware of the somatic presentation of an anxiety disorder in a Filipino American can pave the way to a psychiatric approach.

Adjustment Disorder

This category accounted for 16.2 percent of Filipino American outpatients seen at the Asian Community Mental Health Center in Oakland, California, between 1990 and 1991, second only to mood disorder (see Figure 4.1). In Dr. Sustento-Seneriches's private practice in Pleasanton, California, this diagnosis accounted for 41.3 percent of all Filipino outpatients, a significantly higher percentage than the 3.7 percent of all her outpatients with the same diagnosis in Iloilo, the Philippines (Table 4.1). Distinct immigration and acculturation experiences probably explain the discrepancy between the two settings and cause Filipino American patients to come in with adjustment disorder in Dr. Sustento-Seneriches's California practice. These include

Table 4.1. Comparison Between Diagnosis of Filipino Outpatients Seen in Private Practice in the Philippines and California.

	Iloilo, Philippines		*Pleasanton, California*	
	n = 589	*Percentage*	*n = 75*	*Percentage*
Schizophrenic disorders and other psychoses	220	37.4	12	16.0
Affective disorders	116	19.7	15	20.0
Anxiety disorders	93	15.8	19	25.3
Adjustment disorders	22	3.7	31	41.3
Personality disorders	149	25.3	6	8.0
Substance abuse	62	10.5	0	0.0
Mental retardation	0	0.0	5	6.7

Note: Because a patient may have more than one diagnosis, the percentage totals are greater than 100, and the patient totals appear to exceed the actual number in each population.

losses experienced in the immigration process (loss of extended family, community support, child-rearing support, status, and often financial security), changes in traditional male-female roles, discrepancies in acculturation between first-generation immigrants and American-born later generations, shame (*hiya*) in workplace situations, ignorance of the new country's laws or cultural norms (such as those concerning child or sexual abuse), and legal problems related to immigration (Sustento-Seneriches, 1991).

The adjustment disorders in Dr. Sustento-Seneriches's California practice fall into several main categories: those connected with marital problems, with family problems (especially concerning adolescents), with court-related circumstances, and with work-related circumstances. Symptoms may be disturbed affect (depression, anxiety) and extremes of anger, shame, or guilt. There may also be disturbances in interpersonal, social, school, and work functions, or disturbances in conduct. All emerge within three months of an identifiable psychosocial stressor and remit when the stressors are effectively adapted to. Among Filipino American patients, the stressors are indeed mostly related to the process of immigration and acculturation.

Vignette. *Successful first-generation parents came into Dr. Sustento-Seneriches's office, neatly dressed in suits, with "the family problem" in tow: an adolescent daughter whose hair was dyed a shade of red and who wore pale makeup, black get-up, and boots. The daughter, an A student, had quit a prestigious private high school to join her Caucasian friends in public school. Soon after, her mother started having insomnia and irritability.*

Vignette. *A Filipina, an illegal alien, was fighting the threat of deportation and a resultant separation from her new husband. She reported having crying spells and falling asleep at the wheel.*

Vignette. *A sixty-two-year-old Filipino American male was brought in by his sixty-year-old wife and his younger brother. He and his wife had immigrated from the Philippines eight months before. His complaints were a distressing, persistent insomnia and the preoccupation with thoughts that he was worthless as a provider and might have to return to the Philippines.*

Both he and his wife had come to this country with the dream of sending money to their three grown children in the Philippines, so that they too could eventually immigrate to this country and finally escape what they all perceived as hopeless poverty and the absence of law and order in their home country. Both spouses had worked hard at menial jobs and had been scrupulously saving money toward this goal.

The patient had always been a hard worker and was used to helping needy members of his extended family. He was also used to having a lot of people around him to talk to, give advice to, and be appreciated by. But in his new country, he was often alone in the room he and his wife rented from a couple who also both worked. He himself worked nights, and recently his wife had begun working days. His younger brother lived an hour away. Busy with making a living, husband and wife had no chance to develop friendships. The final straw came when the patient received a call from home, notifying him that his youngest son had to marry his pregnant girlfriend.

He responded to brief individual psychotherapy, with some marital sessions, getting in touch with his feelings about his children and realizing the drastic changes in his life-style. Accordingly, he and his wife worked out a more comfortable life-style, branching out to the Bay Area's vast Filipino American population and their local Catholic church, both of which became strong supports for them.

He consented to use low-dose antidepressants for one week, to counter his insomnia. He was very concerned about drug addiction and flatly refused hypnotics.

Two features differentiate this diagnostic category from the more delineated symptom formation of a major depression or the anxiety disorders: the onset of symptoms within three months of distinct stressors, and the fact that the symptoms disappear when the stressors are resolved or are adapted to.

In treating a patient with this diagnosis, the clinician becomes privy to the immigrant's varied experiences around immigration to a new country and adaptation to a new culture. Diagnosis and proper treatment will require a basic understanding of the psychological processes of these experiences, as well as a knowledge of the cultural strengths that can be accessed for the effective adjustment of patients and their families.

Culture-Bound Syndromes

There are a few defined psychiatric syndromes observed within the Philippine culture, called *culture-bound syndromes*. They are also endemic in the Malay and Chinese cultures, both of which contribute to the unique blend that is the Philippine culture. Strictly speaking, each case can be fitted, however awkwardly, into known Western diagnostic entities; nevertheless, the cultural predispositions, explanations, and presentations are unique, distinctive, and interesting in themselves. Moreover, an understanding of cultural predispositions where personality traits, traditional values, and even child-rearing practices are concerned can greatly aid clinicians in formulating treatment plans and prognosis when patients present with such syndromes.

Running Amok

The first publicized accounts in psychiatry were from among the Muslims of the Philippines, Indonesia, and Malaysia (Zaguirre, 1957); cases have since been reported in Java, New Guinea, Singapore, China, and even the United States. The Malay word *amoq* originally meant "engaging furiously in battle." At present, the concept is broadened enough to describe all kinds of murderous frenzy in a person who uses a deadly weapon. The term *running amok* has now been incorporated into English. With this broader definition, there may be all kinds of psychiatric diagnoses behind the act, seen in all cultures.

Clinical Presentations. In its truest sense, *running amok* refers to a sudden, unprovoked, or disproportionate outburst of wild rage in which a person brandishes a *bolo* (long Philippine knife) or other weapon and kills or maims every person or animal he or she meets while running around in a frenzy. The person is ultimately subdued or killed (Zaguirre, 1957). The Philippine cases first described were of highly religious Muslims in Mindanao, the southernmost group of islands in the Philippine archipelago. Their ritual included shaving their heads before they ran amok to kill "Christian infidels" and thereby assure themselves of eternal salvation. Cases among the Malay cultures in Asia were described later. An episode would begin with a perceived insult to a person's self-esteem (*amor propio*), resulting in the person's helpless shame and humiliation, or it might begin with an infuriatingly frustrating situation in which, again, the person would feel belittled and undeservedly disregarded. The anger would initially be repressed, which would then bring on the first phase: brooding. The individual would become withdrawn, sullen, and preoccupied, with an affect of depression. The second phase—a dramatic, wild, homicidal outburst, compulsive in nature—would last for a few hours (Zaguirre, 1957). The individual, overpowered by rage, might kill as many as ten victims. The last phase would be amnesia with respect to the homicidal frenzy, which the individual would regard in a dissociative fashion. If the person were not killed or did not kill himself or herself in the process of running amok, he or she would eventually calm down, exhausted, and remember nothing of the violent episode (Zaguirre, 1957).

Cultural Explanations. In traditional segments of Philippine society, an episode of running amok can be looked on with sympathetic understanding by the patient's neighbors, who understand it as a reaction to severe frustration or personal humiliation. The widely held theory is that this indulgence is found in a culture that imposes heavy restrictions on adolescents' and adults' aggressive behavior but allows children free rein to express temper tantrums (Zaguirre, 1957). A dominant adult character trait among Filipinos is the inordinate need to maintain smooth interpersonal relationships and resolve disagreements. A common child-rearing practice among traditional Filipinos is to allow for the child's leisurely maturation, accepting temper tantrums as part of being a child. Once the need to conform or show respect toward older members of the family can be understood by the child (as deemed by the tolerant parents), such disciplinary measures as teasing, shaming, repeated admonitions, or outright spanking are used (Sustento-Seneriches and Ladrido-Ignacio, 1983). It may be that people who eventually run amok try hard to suppress their anger and maintain smooth interpersonal relationships but later regress to a state of rage. A culture with popular beliefs in magical or spiritual possession may also make it easy for the individual to attribute aggressive impulses to evil spirits or something beyond his or her control. Therefore, aggression is dissociated or even fanatically sanctioned. Recent immigrants who go through acculturation may be sensitive to feelings of discrimination, especially in public (say, in a job situation), and therefore prone to this syndrome. Dr. Seneriches has seen signs of this narcissistic sensitivity among her Filipino American patients, and Manio (1990) observes among Filipino nurses the same sensitivity to losing face.

Implications. Given the possibility of multiple homicides, running amok is the most dangerous of the culture-bound syndromes discussed in this chapter. In the United States, clinicians must be constantly aware of the possibility that patients have this syndrome, especially if the patients are unacculturated or were raised with the traditional values and child-rearing practices just mentioned. Clinicians must also be alert to precipitating incidents or circumstances construed by patients as shame-inducing and causing narcissistic wounds, as well as to patients' belief in magical possession if they begin to withdraw, brood, and look depressed, even if they do not have any previous psychiatric diagnoses. The use of alcohol or drugs may be an aggravating factor. Of course, this syndrome may coexist with other psychiatric entities like psychosis, affective illness, personality disorder, alcoholism, and drug abuse.

Koro

Koro is usually found in the Filipino-Chinese population, where it is also called *fuk-yeoung*. However, it has also been recorded in Malaysia and even in India. *Fuk-yeoung* is rare. It is an anxiety reaction in which the patient has a desperate, agitated fear that his penis is shrinking and will eventually disappear into his abdomen, at which point he will surely die. In a woman, the vulva and breasts may be the objects of feared retraction. Dr. Sustento-Seneriches has not heard of any cases among women in the Philippines or among Filipino Americans in the United States. Gaw (1993) mentions a case in a Filipino-Chinese male in the United States.

Epidemic attacks of this syndrome have occurred in the

Philippines (among the sugarcane workers in Negros Occidental) and in Singapore, in 1976, when it was rumored that infected pork (from pigs inoculated against swine fever) could cause fatal *koro* in those who ate it. People panicked in Singapore, flooding hospitals and doctors' offices until a panel of experts appeared on television and explained that penile retraction into the abdomen is physiologically impossible and that the condition is nervous in origin (Sustento-Seneriches and Ladrido-Ignacio, 1983).

Clinical Presentations. The symptoms are those of severe anxiety. In panicked desperation, warding off death, the individual and his family will attempt all kinds of physical maneuvers to hold back the "retracting" penis. Contraptions using sticks and strings are often devised.

Cultural Explanations. The Chinese designate the penis as the site of the life force, or *yang*. It has become a popular belief in some parts of the rural Philippines that in a physically ill person the shrinking of the penis is often the prelude to actual death. Other speculations on the origin of *koro* involve culturally distinct castration fears awakened by such common experiences as masturbation, nocturnal emissions, and sexual overindulgence.

Implications. Although this is a rare condition, there is a tendency for groups of people to be affected, as in the Singapore epidemic.

Mali-mali or Latah

This syndrome is found among middle-aged women in native Philippine rural or low-income groups. Other sites are Malaysia and Indonesia.

Clinical Presentations. *Mali-mali* or *latah* consists of coprolalia (curses or culturally "dirty" phrases or words), echopraxia (repetition of actions), or echolalia (repetition of utterances) that can manifest from two sources. One source is the startle reaction, by which a sudden loud noise (say, the honking of a car's horn), an intentionally sudden movement (flailing of the arms), or an intentionally produced sudden sound (a shout) on the part of others can initiate intense fear in the patient. She then stops all normal activities and engages in a series of compulsive, inappropriate motor and verbal reactions. The other source is a purely mimetic reaction, by which she imitates the initiator's movements or utterances. She appears powerless and does what others tell her to do. An essential component of this syndrome is a teasing, laughing audience. The patient may become so embarrassed by her own compulsions that she minimizes her public appearances, which can cause marked personality deterioration if the condition is chronic.

Cultural Explanations. Dissociation and compulsion are part of the mechanics of this disorder. Similar types of this reaction may be seen in younger inhibited and histrionic females and adolescents who briefly exhibit echolalia and echopraxia when startled or embarrassed, as a sort of flirtatious affectation to attract attention. In some of these females, the affectation may gradually progress to a permanent *latah* reaction. The frankness and absence of disguise for sexual imagery are contributing cultural factors that may swamp the histrionic female who uses no other ego defense mechanisms to stave off sexualized issues (Murphy, 1951). Sexualized ventilation and reactions like disrobing in public are among the common manifestations. There may be cultural and social conditions that produce a certain passivity of mind and an unpreparedness for action in the face of sudden stimuli (Yap, 1951).

Implications. Because of the absence in the United States of the aforementioned cultural factors in the patient's community-at-large and the absence of a proximate group (townspeople or a big clan) who can consistently encourage such behavior, it is unlikely that this condition can originate in the United States. If a Filipino American family brings over all its members from the Philippines, however, a rare case of *mali-mali* may be seen here.

Healer's Trance and Possession State

What will be discussed here is an ego-syntonic or psychologically comfortable and accepted state within those afflicted; therefore, it is not considered pathological in the context of Philippine culture, and so it is not commonly discussed as one of the culture-bound syndromes. Still, the cultural aspects make it worth mentioning.

This is a common phenomenon among healers or those considered "spiritually visited." The designation may be a spontaneous one, but it is usually handed down within a family of healers. Individuals go into religious trances or dissociative states, which may start as early as adolescence or young adulthood. They may speak unfamiliar dialects or languages, in different voices. They may preach on religious themes, encourage penance, espouse Catholic spiritual values, or give predictions and healing instructions (Sustento-Seneriches and Ladrido-Ignacio, 1983). In trances, they may take on the characteristics (voices, healing messages, nuances) of religious personae. One commonly observed possession state, for example, takes on the childlike mannerisms of the Santo Niño (the infant Jesus of the Catholic religion). Devotion to the Santo Niño has become widespread in present-day Filipino American communities, and healers in possession states have been espoused by some devotees. Young women in trances may give healing messages from the Virgin Mary.

Differential Diagnoses. These possession states must be differentiated from the pathological states of depersonalization and multiple personality that may be found in psychotics (those with a schizophrenic disorder or bipolar disorder), personality disorders, and dissociative disorders. Physical conditions that may simulate symptoms are alcohol and drug intoxication, epilepsy, brain infections and tumors, febrile states from systemic infections, and some endocrine and metabolic conditions.

Cultural Explanations. The predominantly Catholic population of the Philippine archipelago is ritualistic and openly demonstrative of its religious fervor. Group novenas, processions, group prayers for the Lenten season, and time-designated wakes for the dead are daily phenomena in the Philippine setting and, to a certain extent, are carried to the American setting by Filipino Americans.

Belief in possession by supernatural entities is widespread. There may be possession by spirits inhabiting forests, rocks, caves, seas, rivers, and termite mounds. There may be possession by the spirits of dead relatives (Tan, 1987). Good spirits are harnessed for the healing possession states. Malevolent spirits can cause physical illnesses, which may be countered by advice from the benevolent spirits. This advice may involve rituals that traditional healers use to rid the inflicted person of the effects of malevolent acts, usually in ceremonies attended by the family or clan. Nowadays, traditional healers in healing trances often advise patients to go to doctors for further healing. Many of these healers also demonstrate parapsychic skills, giving their clients predictions and past-life readings.

Conclusion

This discussion should spur more questions and observations, thereby leading to much-needed research and validation of clinical observations. When clinicians are aware of and knowledgeable about their clients' expressions of emotional discomfort, the clinicians will be able to relate to their patients more meaningfully. It is hoped that more meaningful relating will contribute to the closing of the gap between Filipino American patients and our mental health care system.

Chapter 5

Vulnerable Populations and Multicultural Perspectives

This chapter attempts to summarize concerns about the mental health and related concerns of Filipino American children, adolescents, women, and seniors. These groups need special attention because they have been considered at high risk for mental health and other related problems and because they have unique needs that require further investigation. Other concerns, such as AIDS, drug abuse, and marital and immigration problems, will also be discussed.

In January and February of 1992, a workshop and miniforums were held in San Francisco by a group of about seventy Filipino professionals representing public and private agencies, in collaboration with the Department of Public Health of the City and County of San Francisco, the Filipino Mental Health Resource Group, and other agencies. One primary focus of the workshop was the mental health and other health concerns of Filipinos across the life span. The issues and concerns identified by the workshops and miniforums, as well as the recommendations made, are included in this chapter. These issues and concerns are important to the total well-being of the Filipino American community and need urgent attention. The national and international issues need more intensive research and should be considered in any future planning and implementation of mental health programs for Filipino Americans and for Filipinos in other countries.

Children and Adolescents

The majority (more than 60 percent) of Filipino Americans are immigrants. Their immigrant children, as well as first-generation children born in the United States are considered at high risk for identity problems, value conflicts, depression, suicide, "acting out" behavior that may lead to psychoactive substance abuse, teenage pregnancy, accidents, and gang-related activities.

Risk of Physical, Mental and Sexual Abuse

Filipino children are considered family treasures, but they may also become the victims of all forms of abuse. Disciplinary measures practiced in the Philippines (spanking, pinching, "belting," scolding, threatening with spirits of the dead and ghosts, forced kneeling on mango seeds, and being put into rice sacks) may be carried over or may be modified according to the educational level of the parents and whether they come from a rural or an urban area. Common disciplinary measures are usually not considered child abuse, and parents are shocked when they are charged with child abuse. Filipino children in the United States may no longer be threatened with ghosts but may be threatened with being sent back to the Philippines. Instead of being "belted," they may be placed in a closet or a basement for hours at a time. Parents who are not aware of child-abuse regulations and laws in the United States are more inclined to use the "old ways." Unintentional neglect of children is also not uncommon in families where both parents have two or three jobs. Some parents even leave their children in cars while working nearby.

Across cultures, common factors that predispose children to increased probability of maltreatment are high levels of stress, lack of financial resources, unemployment or underemployment, social isolation, an adolescent parent, lack of social support, excessive child-care demands (as with a sick child or many children), poor child-management skills, inappropriate developmental or constitutional or temperamental factors in the child, organic disorders that produce difficult adjustment, overactivity or impulsivity in the child, and emotional illness or past abuse of the parents (Walker and Bonner, 1988). Many of these factors are encountered in Filipino immigrant families.

Del Rosario (1990) cites other distinctive situations among Filipino immigrants that can lead to child abuse:

1. There is often prolonged separation from the parents. It is customary for a Filipino family to immigrate in a piecemeal fashion. One or both parents may come first, with the children coming after the parents have amassed adequate resources. If physical separation occurs during the bonding phase (between infancy and age three), lack of emotional bonding can cause the parents to be detached in their treatment of their children. Del Rosario observes that these children are at risk for developing a borderline personality disorder.
2. The Filipino child-rearing custom of nurturance during infancy and physical discipline later, once the child has grown bigger and is considered able to distinguish between right and wrong, causes infant abuse to be rare. Typically, abused children are older, in the latency stage to adolescence.
3. Preadolescent and adolescent females are liable to be abused by their first-generation parents (usually the mother) when the parents themselves are struggling to balance their "old" value of sexual suppression in adolescence with the explicit sexual representations in the media and in the general U.S. culture. When daughters show interest in boys, such parental abuses as slapping, pulling hair, cutting hair, and locking their daughter in rooms may be observed.
4. When three generations of a family live in the same household, in-laws may present conflicts about discipline. Del Rosario (1990) gives the example of a mother dripping hot candle wax onto her child's hand, to prove to her mother-in-law that there was no laxness about discipline. (The child had been caught stealing from the grandmother's purse.)
5. Parents may believe that it is their right to subdue disobedience by punitive means.

Sexual abuse by parents, siblings, uncles, grandparents, stepparents, and stepsiblings has been increasingly reported among Filipinos in the United States, by comparison with those in the Philippines. However, there are no prevalence studies on sexual abuse of Filipino children and adolescents in either the Philippines or the United States. Many children refuse to disclose sexual abuse because of severe shame and the fear that abusive parents who are also breadwinners may be deported or prosecuted.

> **Vignette.** *L.P. was ten years old when she was brought to the United States by her aunt. She had been living with her grandparents in the Philippines while her parents worked in the United States.*
>
> *When L.P. arrived in the United States, her father was not close to her and rarely talked to her, but later he started sexually abusing her while her mother worked in the evenings. For about four years, L.P. suffered the sexual abuse and never told her mother. She was scared of her father, who threatened to send her back to the Philippines if she told anyone.*
>
> *Then her mother lost her job and had to stay home. At one point, L.P.'s mother became suspicious when the husband got up in the middle of the night and went to L.P.'s room, but she denied the possibility of sexual abuse and pretended not to be aware of it. The wife, too, feared that if she reported her suspicions about her husband, he might lose his job. She and her four children, including L.P., were all dependent on him.*
>
> *The father, who was aware of the consequences of his actions, began bribing L.P. with gifts (watches, more clothes, and so on). L.P. appeared to be the favored of the siblings. She also started to threaten her father with exposure if he did not buy the things she wanted.*
>
> *One day, L.P. saw a TV show on sexual abuse*

and how to report it. She talked to a school counselor about what her father was doing to her. Right away, her father was prosecuted, lost his job, and went to jail.

L.P.'s mother tried to defend her husband, and she blamed L.P. for the consequences. They lost their home, and the mother, with L.P.'s siblings, had to live in her car, moving from place to place for a while until she got another job. L.P. stayed in a home for abused children, under the protection of the Department of Social Services.

Problems in Child Rearing

Since most Filipino Americans are immigrants, they tend to continue the child-rearing practices they learned in their native land. Many were dependent on their *yayas* (nannies) or relatives for child rearing in the Philippines. In the United States they need to work harder and often must leave their children with little supervision. Many children become addicted to television, their most common "companion."

A conflict-provoking cultural gap may appear when older children and adolescents of first-generation parents start becoming assertive about their Westernized inclination toward individuality. Parents and grandparents become deeply hurt and angered by the children's perceived lack of respect and ingratitude. This perception can lead to outright estrangement between parents and children, to acting-out behavior in the children, to depression in the parents, and even to physical abuse.

Risk of Educational and Behavioral Problems and Affective Disorders

In school, Filipinos are generally considered to be members of a "model minority" who are bright, trouble-free, not in need of help, and able to assimilate into the mainstream without much support from the host community. In reality, however, Filipino American children and youth present a different picture. In San

Francisco, for example, they have a higher dropout rate (26 percent) than other Asians (8 percent), although that rate is lower than the rates for Latinos (32 percent), whites (33 percent), and African Americans (29 percent).

There is a clear need for biculturally sensitive teachers and teaching materials. Tagalog is the dominant language of instruction in the early grades in the Philippines. While immigrants have also learned English in the Philippine schools, they still struggle with spoken American English.

One public school in the San Francisco district has Filipino Americans constituting 42 percent of its students, but the school has only about 2 percent Filipino American teachers (Catubig, 1992). Lack of adequate Filipino American role models in school aggravates the problems of identity and self-concept in students whose parents do not become adequately involved in their children's education. The parents were not expected to participate actively in the Philippine educational system the way they are in their new country. Besides, their priorities are mostly focused on making a living.

Of a total of 2,510 suspensions during one school year in the San Francisco district, 4 percent involved Filipino American youth. The major reasons for suspension were assault, battery, or menace (46 percent); use or possession of a firearm or other weapon (18 percent); disruption or defiance of school activities (13 percent); grafitti and school property damage (12 percent); stealing (7 percent); and other antisocial behavior or tobacco use (3 percent). There have also been instances of cutting classes, failing grades, gang-related activities, attempted or actual running away, attempted suicide, teenage pregnancy, and substance abuse.

Middle school Filipino American students in San Francisco, compared to other Asian groups, have the highest rate of suicidal thoughts (34 percent) and suicide attempts (21 percent). High rates of teenage pregnancy have also been reported by comparison to other groups. For instance, of the 2.9 percent births in San Francisco in 1987 that occurred in school-age teens, 1.9 percent were to Filipino Americans, 1.4 percent were to other Asians, and 1.1 percent were to non-Hispanic whites. (This rate was lower than the rates for Latino and African American teenagers.)

Vignette. *G.S. was a charming sixteen-year-old Filipina in her junior year of high school in San Francisco. She was born in a rural area of the Philippines. Her family brought her to the United States when she was eight years old. Her father is described as very strict and her mother as overprotective. She was not allowed to attend parties and was always asked to come home early from school.*

She went to a public school, where she became a member of the barkada *(peer group) composed of eight other immigrant girls. The* barkada *started dating boys, mostly Filipino-American.*

G.S. became more disobedient of her parents. At times, she was physically punished and scolded by her father for coming home late. She was also caught cutting classes when she went to a movie with her barkada *and their boyfriends.*

When G.S. found out that she was pregnant, she became so scared that she ran away from home. Her Filipino boyfriend wanted the baby, but G.S. was thinking about having an abortion.

When the two sets of parents learned about the pregnancy, they decided to let their children marry and continue going to school. It was discovered that three other members of the barkada *had also become pregnant. The young women said that they were not taught about contraceptives and never expected to get pregnant. G.S. finished high school but was not able to attend college because of her baby.*

Vignette. *M.T. was considered the brightest student in his eighth-grade class. His parents had come from Manila and immigrated to the United States after the declaration of martial law by President Marcos.*

M.T. was born in San Francisco, the youngest of four siblings. His parents always wanted M.T. to top the class, and they expected him to get a scholarship to a Catholic high school. He was rarely allowed to pursue social activities because he was expected to study. He resented this family pressure to achieve but felt obliged to live up to his parents' expectations.

M.T. was not able to maintain his A average when his father got sick and lost his job. He became depressed and attempted suicide by jumping from a three-story school building. At first, his parents were hesitant to take M.T. to a psychiatrist because of shame, and because they thought M.T. was not crazy. Upon the advice of their parish priest, however, they brought him to a Filipino child psychiatrist. M.T. was able to continue high school.

Barkada *Versus Gang*

The *barkada* is a Filipino peer group that is mainly social in nature. The members usually have common interests, such as sports, and they organize such activities as parties and outings or help one another in school or at work. Most of the members come from the same social class or the same school and may have many traits and characteristics in common.

The term *gang* mainly refers to a group with mostly antisocial and criminal activities. A *barkada* that started with mostly social activities may become a gang when the members become involved in illegal and antisocial activities.

An investigation conducted by Enriquez (1990) in Honolulu suggests that the gang problem among Filipino American youth is neither an ethnic nor an immigrant problem. The gang problem is common across cultures. The most common age group is fourteen to twenty-four. Males usually join gangs, but girls may also join. Some girlfriends of gang members form gangs to support their boyfriends. The common demographic profile of gang members is that they are usually school dropouts; some may be repeaters, mostly in public schools. The Filipino gang members studied by Enriquez in Honolulu mostly lived in crowded households, with several relatives and other families, and in crowded areas with inadequate recreational activities. The parents of the gang members had come from rural areas in the Philippine and had two to three low-paying or nonprofessional jobs. The common demographic profile of Filipino juvenile delinquents has similarities to the profile of gang members in Honolulu (Carlota and Carlota, 1983). According to Enriquez (1990), Filipinos are overrepresented in Honolulu gangs, by comparison with other groups.

Many Filipino American gang members report that their main reason for joining gangs was protection against other gangs. Others claim that they became gang members because they did not get enough love and attention at home or were bored and had nothing else to do. Some were forced to join because other members of their *barkadas* started joining gangs.

Behaviors identified as indicators that a youth is at risk for gang membership include poor performance in school, truancy, lack of hobbies, nothing to do during leisure time, problems at home, frequent negative contact with police officers, living in a neighborhood where gangs exist, having friends who are gang members or in gang attire, having tattoos, and dressing in gang-style clothes.

Men, Women, and Marriage

Changes in sex roles brought on by the immigration experience are liable to affect marital equilibrium and create problems in the individual spouses and consequently in the children. The outwardly dominant and sexualized stance of the Filipino male, with the double standard of morality and *machismo* brought in by Spanish influence, has been discussed by Sustento-Seneriches and Ladrido-Ignacio (1983). It has already been noted that the Filipino family is bilateral in structure, neither patriarchal nor matriarchal, and that Filipino women are highly regarded in economic matters. Traditionally, they hold the purse strings. They do not walk paces behind their husbands, and they are more vocal socially and in public than more traditional Asian women. Yet they also accept the double standard of morality and suffer their husbands' extramarital affairs, receiving community and family support and religious approval for their patience and suffering.

The immigration experience may bring loss of social status (especially when there are visa problems), encounters with racial discrimination, financial difficulties, underemployment, or unemployment, all of which weigh heavily on the husband's sense of his own masculinity. Other losses may include loss of clan and family networks of support, including the husband's network of male friends (as in his hometown *barkada*) and the wife's traditional hired help with household chores and child rearing. There may be isolation as well. Marital difficulties may include sexual problems, lack of communication, separation or divorce, alcohol abuse, spouse and child abuse, and extramarital affairs. In such marriages, depressive and anxiety disorders are quite common in men and women alike.

> **Vignette.** *A couple immigrated with their two-year-old son and hoped for a better life in their new country. They settled in a big city, with no known friends and no extended-family members. The wife, a nurse, took several jobs in nursing homes and prepared for exams to update her license. Her husband, who had been a high-ranking lawyer in his Philippine hometown, was underemployed and was also preparing to update his license. When he did not pass his exam but his wife passed hers, he became despondent and then abusive toward his wife and son. The couple finally came for marital therapy a year later, after the wife began an affair with a co-worker.*

Indeed, a wife's extramarital affair is not an uncommon reason for a Filipino American couple to seek marital counseling. The husband, initially unwilling to consider therapy, may even initiate it when his wife acts out her discontent in a serious friendship with another man or in an outright extramarital affair (Sustento-Seneriches, 1991).

Nearly a quarter of a million Asian and Pacific women have married American servicemen overseas since World War II. In the Philippines, many of the wives had lived in and around the military bases, and a considerable number had been prostitutes;

the bases dominated the local economies and fostered exploitation of women and children. The marital relationship might start out as basic domination on the husband's part and dependence on the wife's, who might play the stereotyped role of Asian Pacific wife—obedient, quiescent, and passive. These women, in the first stage of immigration, indeed become quite dependent on their husbands, relying on them financially, socially, and emotionally. Many cannot communicate well in English, and all are uprooted from their families, friends, and familiar culture. The military life—with its frequent moves, its emphasis on authority and use of physical force, and its high rate of alcohol abuse—adds to the wives' colonial mentality, dependence, high regard for authority, and fear of deportation. The stage is set for family violence and various marital problems. "Mail-order brides" from the Philippines, with their utter dependence on their husbands, their inherent colonial mentality, and their husbands' expectations of the stereotyped Asian woman, are also liable to be abused and to have other marital and emotional difficulties.

Partners in an interracial marriage also face cultural adjustments on both sides. In addition, the Filipino spouse must go through the process of acculturation. Cultural differences are liable to come up in communication, sex roles, expectations of the marriage, child-rearing practices, issues with in-laws, and social and financial situations. Sexual abuse of stepchildren has also been reported in such marriages.

A common child-rearing quandary in an interracial marriage is the Filipino spouse's complete nurturance of the child, including the practice of allowing the child to sleep in the parents' bed. This is traditionally the time for bonding with the child in the Filipino culture, which emphasizes interdependence among family members. But this is also the time for encouraging autonomy and independence in the American culture.

The Filipino spouse's continued interdependence with his or her own family of origin is a common source of conflict between spouses, as is the American spouse's tendency to be frank and direct in communication. Divorce is not sanctioned in Catholic Philippine society and is mostly a very painful process when undergone by a Filipino American immigrant.

The Elderly

Elderly Filipino Americans have constituted 26.7 percent (the largest subgroup) of the Asian American elderly population since 1980, followed by the Chinese (26.6 percent), the Japanese (24.7 percent), Asian Indians (14.6 percent), the Koreans (4.2 percent), the Vietnamese (2.2 percent), and other Asians (1 percent) (U.S. Bureau of Census, 1988). The number of Filipino American elders is expected to increase tremendously, especially with the influx of Filipino veterans and the expected modifications of U.S. immigration laws concerning veterans. The majority of Filipino elders live in the warmer states, such as California, Hawaii, and Florida.

The *manongs*—usually single males from rural areas, with little education, who were recruited to work on farms and plantations and in canneries—continue to be at risk for mental health problems, along with elderly newcomers who have been sponsored by their adult immigrant sons and daughters. The newcomers are considered important family resources as babysitters or housesitters and for what they may be able to contribute financially because of their social security benefits.

Risk of Affective Disorders and Alcoholism

Loss of the usual supports, as well as isolation, role reversals or changes, and unfulfilled expectations, may predispose the elderly to depression and anxiety disorders, as well as to alcohol abuse. Filipino American elders who used to have many friends and companions at home in the Philippines find themselves left alone at home in the new country, or left with young children to care for. They have limited opportunities to move around in the community because they usually must depend on their children for transportation or have limited knowledge of the transportation system. Sometimes their adult sons and daughters do not allow them to leave home, for fear that they will get lost or attacked in the street.

Male Filipino American elders are especially prone to alcoholism. They feel bored staying home alone and spend their lonely hours drinking. When depressive symptoms start and when the effects of alcohol abuse or dependence begin may be difficult to delineate. Some elderly people may also be prone to suicidal ideation and attempts.

> **Vignette.** *Mr. S., a retired schoolteacher from the Philippines, was sent for by his eldest son and came to the United States at the age of sixty-eight. When he joined his son's family, he was expected to take care of a two-year-old grandson. His main job was to take his grandson to and from a day-care center and take care of him until the parents arrived in the evening.*
>
> *Mr. S. became very lonely and depressed. He missed his old friends, with whom he had played mah-jonng. He also missed the cockfight on Sundays. He described his new home and community as being like a "cemetery." He became so depressed that he thought of killing himself. He also developed insomnia, poor appetite, irritability, loss of weight, and guilt that he might not be able to live up to the expectations of his son.*
>
> *When he began to complain of frequent headaches and chest pains, he was referred from a medical clinic to the Filipino Depression Research Project in San Francisco. He was treated for his depression and medical problems, and family counseling was initiated by a Filipino counselor.*

Risk of Physical, Mental, and Financial Abuse

Filipino elders are usually well respected and cared for, but the changes and stress experienced by families predispose some members to abuse of the elders. For instance, an adult daughter experiencing financial difficulty may keep her father's social security check and threaten him with abandonment when he confronts her. In one reported case, an elderly woman was left in an unfamiliar place after a quarrel with her adult daughter.

In another instance, an elderly woman was physically abused by her alcoholic adolescent grandson. With no one to turn to, with limited knowledge of mental health resources, and with the fear of sharing their experiences because of strong shame and the stigma associated with mental health counseling, Filipino American elders are at risk for serious mental health disorders.

Access to Medical Care and Community Resources

It is common knowledge that Filipino American elders rarely go to clinics, with their unfamiliar staff, in the early stages of an illness. They prefer to use home-made remedies, medicines from the Philippines or from friends, and prescription drugs from the Philippines, with no current medical supervision. Spiritual healing, prayers, faith healing, and herbs are still parts of the healing practices of Filipino elders. With their limited knowledge of the U.S. medical care system, and with unfamiliar clinic personnel who may not understand their accents, Filipino American elders delay medical consultations or do not consult medical and mental health professionals at all.

AIDS and Substance Abuse

Filipino Americans have the highest percentage (39 percent) of AIDS cases among Asians and Pacific Islanders in San Francisco. It is highly probable that the true number of AIDS cases is underreported because of shame, stigma, and fear of deportation and rejection.

Filipino Americans tend to have low knowledge about AIDS. Self-identified gay and bisexual Filipino men do display high knowledge about AIDS, but this knowledge tends not to be translated into appropriate safe-sex practices. Certain beliefs prevail, such as that AIDS is transmitted by mosquito bites and razors and can be treated with penicillin, like gonorrhea or syphilis. For example, a Filipina prostitute who was asked if she was scared of AIDS answered, "I am not really that scared about AIDS, as long as I have penicillin." There is an urgent need to educate the Filipino community on AIDS, taking cultural background and religious values into account.

The increasing use of psychoactive substances, especially among Filipino American youth and young adults, is alarming. Many of the substance abusers started using street drugs (such as marijuana) even before they came to the United States. Some have progressed from marijuana and beer to heroin and crack cocaine. Environmental and socioeconomic stressors, conflicts with family members, peer pressure, and job pressure and demands are among the common predisposing factors that lead Filipino Americans to the use of psychoactive substances.

Cross-Cultural Perspectives in Forensic Psychiatry

The role of the mental health clinician dealing with legal problems among Filipino Americans is to bridge the two cultures. On the one hand, there is a need to interpret and explain the U.S. legal system to Filipino American clients. For example, for new immigrants and unacculturated Filipino Americans, the American jury system must be differentiated from the familiar Philippine legal system, which has a sole presiding judge. Communication with predominantly non-Filipino judges, lawyers, social workers, and court personnel must be sorted out and explicitly explained, lest it be misinterpreted and reacted to inappropriately. On the other hand, the mental health clinician must also interpret and explain the presentations and backgrounds of Filipino American clients to the American legal system. This chapter deals mainly with the latter aspect of this task.

Language and Communication

A very real and intricate language barrier exists for Filipino Americans. It must be remembered that the Philippines is an archipelago with diverse regions and more than one hundred distinct dialects (Ignacio, 1991). Filipinos from the Muslim south cannot understand the northern mountain province's dialect. On the island of Panay, dialects may shift every forty miles or so. Those emigrating to the United States after early adolescence retain their accents. Those who come from certain regions will mix their *p*'s and *f*'s. Vowel sounds (long *e*'s, short *e*'s, short *i*'s) can be hard to pronounce. Idiomatic expressions also differ between North American English and the Filipino languages.

Adding to the urgency and frustration of present realities in the California courts is the fact that there are only a few registered Filipino court interpreters. Experts in the language can explain how prefixes and suffixes change an active verb into a passive verb. In a legal situation, where guilt and responsibility for a crime must be determined, the implications can be far-reaching. When a literal English translation of a Filipino phrase is shouted out in a public display of anger, major misinterpretation may occur.

> **Vignette.** *A recent Filipina immigrant was feeling quite content in her job of two years. Unexpectedly, she was approached by her immediate supervisor's boss, who advised her to apply for a lower-ranking job in a different department "because of future layoffs" in her own department. To add to her consternation, the Filipina discovered that her own supervisor was not aware of any planned layoffs.*
>
> *She spent restless nights feeling helpless and frustrated, not knowing where to turn. A few days later, she was handed a document to sign, which acknowledged that her letter of resignation had been accepted. But she had written no such letter.*
>
> *Feeling unjustifiably manipulated, she slammed the letter down on her desk and verbally lashed out with literal English translations of Filipino expressions of anger: "Your day will come! God will take care of you!" In her native language, this is quite a passive expression and literally puts matters into God's hands.*
>
> *A few evenings later, the police barged into her house while she was putting her infant son to sleep and hauled her off to jail on charges of terrorism. The company, it turned out, had received a highly threatening letter, which the worker vehemently denied writing.*

These considerable language difficulties, coupled with cultural traits that may be misconstrued as inscrutability or even sociopathy (what with the client's ever-pleasant countenance), can lead to drastic mistakes in the psychological assessment of unacculturated Filipino Americans. Court-ordered psychological tests must be conducted with a Filipino interpreter, preferably one who speaks the client's dialect and has knowledge of psychological tests. Some psychological testing materials do have Filipino (Tagalog) versions, but there is a dearth of Filipino American psychologists who can administer these tests.

> **Vignette.** *An unacculturated Filipino American male had not completed the elementary grades in the rural Philippines, where he grew up, and was being tried in a criminal case. Initial standard psychological tests gave the diagnostic impression of a highly disorganized state, even a psychosis or a schizophrenic disorder. Closer scrutiny by Filipino-speaking clinicians showed a depressed first-generation Filipino American male who could not communicate well in English, offered frequent concrete interpretations of the many questions asked him, and maintained a polite, smiling, roundabout way of communicating, sometimes even fabricating details that he thought would please the interviewer.*

Nonverbal cues are often used to express potent messages that are contrary to verbal cues. Here, an understanding of Filipino cultural traits and values becomes a necessity. The predominant need to maintain smooth interpersonal relations can cause the client to smile, conform, and placate, especially in the face of the anxiety, resentment, and disagreement that a legal situation is fraught with. Moreover, the sensitivity to being shamed in public, and the need to fit in and be accepted, added to the aforementioned traits, can produce a seemingly passive client whose veracity and reliability may appear shaky. He or she may even appear to be intentionally hiding facts from a Caucasian audience used to stating facts and feelings as they are, without resorting to euphemisms, roundabout explanations, or whatever other maneuvers can soften a dissenting view or hide shameful anxiety. The client may smile and nod as a lawyer is talking, seeming to agree. In fact, however, the client may be nodding to the person's right to say what is being said, not necessarily to the content of what is said.

Child-Rearing Practices

A big part of the mental health clinician's job is to explain what are considered normal or culturally acceptable traits and values in the Filipino culture. A common scenario involves the utter unfamiliarity of new immigrants with American laws on sexual abuse, especially children.

> **Vignette.** *A young Filipino father had immigrated to this country to find a job, save some money, and pave the way for his wife and children to join him. He started by working in the manager's office of an apartment complex. Because of his longing for his own children, and because Filipino parenting encourages physical demonstrations of affection, he soon became very popular with the children who played on the lawn outside the manager's office.*
>
> *One day, a very young boy went to his office and, as usual, played near him. Soon the boy indicated that he urgently needed to urinate. As he was used to doing in the Philippines, the man carried the little boy to the lawn, helped him open his trousers, and allowed him to urinate on the bushes. From the second floor, an elderly Caucasian couple observed these proceedings with fearful indignation and promptly called the police. The bewildered man found himself in jail, accused of sexual molestation.*

First-generation Filipino parents do not think twice about spanking and beating their misbehaving children in public. In this country, such actions are grounds enough for neighbors to make a report of child abuse.

Child-custody evaluations and divorce proceedings are also unfamiliar ground to new immigrants, since divorce is not allowed in the Philippines. The clinician is often required to explain these processes.

Legal Issues in the Workplace

Another major arena for legal problems among Filipino immigrants is the workplace (Manio, 1990). There are claims for workmen's compensation. These involve depression, anxiety stemming from such disabilities as back injuries and injuries from accidents. The common cause of emotional decompensation is loss of livelihood. After all, economic reasons are among the top reasons for immigration in this group. There may be posttraumatic stress disorder from robberies at work. Complaints of discrimination and illegal termination also abound (Sustento-Seneriches, 1991), and many cultural factors contrive to make this so (see Chapter Six).

> **Vignette.** *A Filipino physician who was sponsored in this country by a hospital felt such a strong sense of gratitude and obligation that he decided to stay in the same job even when he was offered advancement elsewhere. He sensed that the hospital would be greatly understaffed for the next two years, and that this would be an opportunity for him to repay his debt of gratitude.*

> **Vignette.** *A Filipino American employee for a big company considered the company "his own" (as part of his concept of extended family) and worked overtime of his own accord. He even had his wife help him out with company business during weekends, and he turned down weekend social invitations. When he was reprimanded by his supervisors in front of others and lost face, he started having severe chest pains and was rushed to the hospital.*

Unacculturated Filipino employees expect their displays of gratitude to be appreciated and rewarded with promotions and raises. When these outcomes do not occur, they feel a deep sense of personal hurt and injustice.

Frankness, open compliments, and assertiveness are not encouraged by the Philippine culture, which emphasizes humility in public. Therefore, unacculturated Filipino administrators may be viewed as cold if they do not give compliments, and they may become embarrassed when they are given compliments (Manio, 1990). *Hiya* and losing face in public, coupled with personalism, can create explosive situations for Filipino immigrants in the workplace. They readily quit or become emotionally distressed when they feel public embarrassment, and many workman's compensation cases have arisen from such situations.

In the workplace, respect for elders and authorities is highly valued. An unacculturated female Filipino American supervisor who feels she is shown disrespect in public by her subordinates may react more intensely than her Western counterpart would. When she cannot express her hurt, because of her fear of losing her job or because she is obligated to maintain smooth interpersonal relationships, emotional problems may very well set in. If her expertise is questioned in public, the same repercussions—shame, hurt, and emotional problems—can occur. Those evaluating her for worker's compensation may not be able to ascertain the causes of her trouble if they are not aware of the cultural factors involved. These clients are often wrongly seen as malingerers, which only adds to their frustration and shame. Moreover, Filipino American employees may place tremendous value on their families' honor, so that when their own integrity or knowledge is publicly questioned, they may decompensate emotionally or fight back by suing to vindicate the family's honor. Western lawyers may not comprehend the intensity or rationality of these reactions.

Another pertinent cultural trait that can affect the legal situation is the sense of fatalism or reliance on God. The resulting passive stance may be exasperating to a well-meaning lawyer. These clients may see their legal predicaments as spiritual tests, or as retribution for past wrongdoing, and calmly accept them.

Conclusion

The rough road of acculturation can well lead the immigrant into a legal maze. Clashes of cultural values, outlooks, and expectations in the workplace, home, school, and community may lead to legal difficulties and courtroom scenarios. Ignorance of the laws and the legal system in the adopted country further confounds the immigrant, who in turn can appear baffling to legal personnel. This can lead to mutual misperceptions.

In such cases, understanding cross-cultural issues becomes highly valuable, as is true in all aspects of mental health care involving the new varied cultures that are fast transforming the American profile.

Chapter 6

The Traditional Filipino Family

From a clinical perspective, a knowledge of Filipino family dynamics will strongly influence accuracy in assessment and the efficacy in treatment of this population. The traditional Filipino family consists of the nuclear family, composed of the father-husband, mother-wife, and child/children, as well as the bilateral extended family, which includes the relatives of both husband and wife. it is not unusual for close ties to be maintained with first, second, and third cousins and their families. The family is the main source of the emotional, moral, and financial support of the members. Interdependence is the norm among the family members.

The father is considered the head of the nuclear family, but the mother mainly governs the household. Generally, the father is responsible for supporting the nuclear family, but he usually gives his earnings to the wife, who budgets the family income and gives an allowance to the father. While the mother is mainly responsible for child rearing (which is also shared among extended-family members, like grandparents), she is not commonly prevented from earning additional income for the family. Female patients in Iloilo, Philippines, give "housewife" as their occupation on intake forms less frequently than their counterparts in New York state; the Filipina women consider themselves businesswomen even if their added income comes merely from selling a few pigs per year. These women see themselves in a partnership role beyond domestic activities. The father is expected to help discipline the children and to do some major household chores, like repairing broken furniture or mowing the lawn. The mother is primarily responsible for the social, religious, health, and educational activities of the nuclear family. Major decisions, such as buying a house, selecting the type of health intervention or type of doctor to be consulted, changing residence, or changing jobs, are usually made in consultation with the members of the nuclear and the extended family.

Older siblings are expected to help with the parents' responsibilities in the family, such as child rearing, and may also discipline younger siblings. In the absence of a parent, the eldest brother generally takes over the father's responsibilities, and the eldest daughter carries on the mother's responsibilities. A special sibling group is also significant in the Filipino family (Andres, 1987). Alliances among siblings make shared responsibilities less of a burden. In the absence of parents, siblings become more supportive of each other.

The Filipino household consists of the nuclear family and may also include the grandparents or a widowed grandparent, an unmarried sibling, or any member of the bilateral extended family.

The nuclear family has a nonconsanguineous extended-family kinship system. Through Christian (particularly Catholic) rituals of baptism, confirmation, and marriage, kinship is acquired between godparents and the parents of the baptized or confirmed child, or between the parents of the newlyweds, as well as between the godfather or godmother or marriage sponsors and the godchildren (baptized or confirmed children). The ritual kinship system helps ensure synergistic social, emotional, and economic support among the godparents, the parents, and the godchildren. The godparents are also expected to provide emotional, moral, and some financial support to the godchildren, as needed.

When the members of the Filipino nuclear family or extended family migrate to the United States, they usually live with relatives during the first few months or years until they find jobs or can afford to rent an apartment or, at times, until they have saved enough to buy a house. Very rarely do Filipino immigrants become homeless. There is almost always a relative, a fellow Filipino, or a hometown friend who will help the immigrant find a place to stay.

Adult members of the nuclear or extended family may continue to live with the nuclear family or relatives until they get married or, at times, even after they get married. Conflicts with in-laws may force the married couple to separate, or they may live on their own once they have enough resources to have their own household.

It is also uncommon for Filipino immigrants to live in a place where they have no relatives. If there are no relatives, however, they easily find a surrogate family or surrogate relatives, specially close friends without blood relations. Such relationships are formed in work settings, in neighborhoods, or in social and recreational activities. It is common for the children to call adult surrogate-family members by such names as "auntie" or "uncle," "grandpa" or "grandma."

Family ties and obligations continue even after marriage, transfer of residence, change in social status, and immigration. Filipinos who live abroad are expected to continue supporting their elderly parents or to help meet the educational and financial needs of siblings or members of the extended family. When a member of the nuclear or extended family is sick or dies in the Philippines, the Filipinos abroad are expected to help pay the hospital bills and doctors' fees, to send medicines, and to send money to help pay funeral expenses. They are also expected to go home to the Philippines to visit sick parents or attend funerals. Inability to live up to family expectations causes much distress and may contribute to the development of depressive disorders.

A popular indigenous Filipino legend on the origin of mankind is that woman and man emerged together from a bamboo cylinder when it split because of the pecking of a bird. At the very beginning, there was equality between Filipino women and men. In precolonial times, women were allowed to become village chieftains. In modern times, Corazon Aquino became the first woman president of the Philippines. By comparison with other Asian women in general, women in the Philippines have higher standing, both in the home and in the community. They have more civil rights. They can own, buy, or inherit property and can have their own businesses. In terms of economic opportunities, Filipino American women have the highest labor-force participation rate (more than 70 percent) among Asian American women (but do earn less than Chinese, Japanese, and Korean full time workers; see Gardner, Robey, and Smith, 1989). Filipino wives are expected to be faithful to their husbands, but men are traditionally tolerated by society and by the family when they have mistresses or become unfaithful, since they are perceived as only trying to prove their *machismo*. This outlook is drastically changing in Philippine urban areas, and certainly among Filipino American wives.

Traditional Values

The present Filipino culture is an integrated mixture of Malayan, Chinese, Indonesian, Asian Indian, Spanish, and American influences, which all contribute to its diversity. Many Filipino characteristics, traits, and values are similar to those of other cultures, particularly Asian and Hispanic. What is significant is the modal differences among different groups, as well as between subethnic groups within the same culture (Sue and Morishima, 1982). For example, Filipinos value respect for elders more than Americans do. This does not mean that Americans do not respect their elders, but the degree to which this value is manifested in the Filipino culture is much greater than in the mainstream American culture. The greater the modal differences between two cultures, the more significant those values and traits are to a particular culture. Common Filipino traits and values have been recorded by many social scientists through observation, use of questionnaires, administration of psychological tests to certain groups, and generalizations from Filipino legends, proverbs, stories, poems, and songs (Sustento-Seneriches and Ladrido-Ignacio, 1983). An awareness of these traits and values is necessary in assessing norms and the meaning of behavior among Filipino American clients.

Enriquez's indigenous personality theory (1990) stresses shared identity, on a strongly equal basis with one's fellow men, as the core value or basic root of all Filipino values. This basic value is crucial to survival within an agricultural island economy where natural calamities (typhoons, ongoing volcanic phenomena) are the norm. Enriquez identifies the following traditional Filipino values:

- Interaction with others on an equal basis
- Sensitivity to and regard for others
- Respect and concern
- Helping out
- Understanding and making up for others' limitations
- Rapport and acceptance

All these values emphasize sensitivity and close attention to other people and to interrelationships. The spirit of comradeship, based on unselfishness and good faith, is also a principal element cited by Agoncillo and Guerrero (1987). Collective helping out is seen in the traditional townspeople's joint effort to carry a neighbor's hut from one location to another. Sharing one's winnings, sharing surplus food, faithfulness, and togetherness in need or in plenty are other regional values related to helping (Enriquez, 1990). Sensitivity to others' unspoken messages, through actions or euphemisms, is valued in the service of smooth interpersonal relationships.

Cultural Characteristics and Traits

Major cultural characteristics that affect Filipino behavior include familism, authoritarianism, personalism, religiosity, adaptability, and colonial mentality. A number of other traits also have an influence.

Familism

Like other Asian and like Hispanics, Filipinos greatly value their families, with the family's needs and welfare coming before those of the individual or community. The Filipino's concept of self is strongly identified with his or her nuclear and extended family. Since childhood, the importance of loyalty and interdependence among Filipino family members, rather than the total independence valued by Western culture, has been inculcated. Family problems are significant stressors that can trigger mental disorders. A family member's mental illness is identified as the family's illness, which causes shame and stigmatizes the family. It is common for a Filipino patient to be accompanied by a family member, and for the accompanying relative to be present when the patient is seen or examined by a doctor for the first time.

Authoritarianism

Respect for authority figures and elders is highly valued. Younger people are expected not to disagree openly with their elders or to talk back to their parents. This value is often the cause of conflicts between first-generation parents and their second-generation adolescent children.

Generally, Filipinos value people in authority, like doctors, priests, employers, government officials, and those with higher education. They believe that they can depend on such parent figures, and they rarely question or disagree with them. Filipino workers, for instance, seldom disagree with their bosses; instead, they try hard to please them. Filipino patients generally regard their attending physicians as second to God, and they expect their doctors to do things for them, sometimes beyond their real expertise. For instance, they ask for legal advice or for help with immigration papers. They also tend to follow doctors' recommendations but are afraid or ashamed to ask questions.

Personalism

Jocano (1981) has used the term *personalism* to stress the personal quality of Filipinos' interactions. Filipinos have a tendency to relate to persons rather than to agencies or institutions. For example, Filipino clients prefer to go to a clinic or a hospital where they know at least some staff members. Recognizing this characteristic is important in the delivery of mental health services. The patient may stop going to a clinic if the staff changes, for example, and so the patient should be introduced to new staff members or clinicians before the transfer of services. Filipinos also prefer personal referrals to a clinic or a hospital, no matter how efficient or effective another clinic may be. A telephone call is preferred to a letter, and the personal touch is appreciated more than a sophisticated laboratory examination. After good rapport has been established, Filipinos often ask doctors or clinicians personal questions and expect at least some answers.

Because Filipinos have a strong personalistic view of the world, they have difficulties separating objective and impersonal events from their own emotional involvement. For example, given constructive criticism in relation to their jobs, they tend to take the criticism personally, as an affront to their self-esteem. Given sincere appreciation for a job well done, however, they have a hard time accepting it, thinking that special attention or affection is being given. Extreme personalism, considered one of the weaknesses of the Filipino character, promotes the tendency not to strictly follow impersonal rules and regulations and to give money or gifts in order to receive special favors in business transactions. The personal approach is almost a requirement for an effective work or business relationship. Personal connections are also considered important in getting jobs and promotions and in receiving or giving services.

Religiosity

Religion is central to Filipino life. It is closely interrelated with the physical, emotional, and mental aspects of well-being. It enables people to face reality with strength and optimism. The Filipinos' profound faith in God makes them accept adversity without many deleterious effects on their self-esteem. Their natural religiosity is a vital resource in helping them cope with their stressors. It also has a stabilizing effect on their lives in times of distress.

Religious and spiritual factors are considered important in explaining both causes of and possible remedies for illnesses.

Faith healing continues to be part of the indigenous healing system, especially for illnesses considered incurable. Because the church considers suicide a mortal sin, the suicide rate among religious Filipinos is generally lower than among those without religion. Many Filipino immigrants consider the Church to be a part of their extended family that provides them moral, emotional, and spiritual support, especially when the nuclear family is not available. Movements like the charismatic movement and prayer meetings are also important segments of the religious support system among immigrant Filipinos.

The predominantly Catholic Filipinos have the tendency to practice their religion in a concrete and personal manner. Religious practices include going to church on Sundays and holidays, saying the rosary, praying novenas, and observing Church rites (baptism, confirmation, weddings, reconciliations; lighting candles and using religious articles at home and in vehicles). Many Filipino Catholics also have personal patron saints, whom they ask for special favors. For instance, they ask St. Jude to intercede, especially in desperate cases, and praying the novena to the Mother of Perpetual Help is a common practice when a professional is taking a licensure examination.

With great confidence in God's mercy, Filipinos tend to be readily resigned to their fate. They also have the tendency to become passive and patient and are prone to being exploited and oppressed. Accepting suffering as a spiritual offering is a coping mechanism when events are beyond their control.

Filipino Catholicism is also based on folk Christianity, with its roots in pre-Spanish paganism. It has its accompanying superstitious beliefs (Andres, 1987). This so-called split-level Christianity is characterized by the existence of two opposing value systems in the same person, although he or she is neither bothered by nor guilty about the existence of this inconsistency (Bulatao, 1964). For example, some Filipinos consider themselves practicing Catholics but at the same time believe in fortune telling and other superstitious practices.

Adaptability

Another outstanding Filipino characteristic is the ability to adapt to different situations and adjust to varying environments. Filipino immigrants are found in many countries, and they strive to adapt to changes and difficulties with resourcefulness and creativity. They also have high tolerance for what is unknown or uncertain. Their great faith in God helps them accept sudden change, tragedy, and uncertainty. With their good sense of humor, they can laugh at themselves during times of misfortune as well as during their triumphs.

Colonial Mentality

This has been one of the legacies of colonization. Oppressed and exploited for four centuries by their colonizers, Filipinos learned to think of themselves as inferior to their colonizers and to value Western looks, goods, and culture as superior to their own. The colonial mentality has eroded the Filipino national consciousness and cultural identity. Filipino immigrants bring with them this colonial mentality, which can impede their upward socioeconomic mobility and political assertiveness in their new country (Lott, 1976).

Hiya

A form of social control is *hiya*—shame or propriety (Enriquez, 1990). This control is probably most effective in a closely knit society, in a clan, on an island, or in a closed-in region. There is concern for social approval and acceptance by others and the need to belong to a group. Behavior depends on what others will say, think, or do. Moreover, while growing up traditionally, the Filipino child has been watchfully taken care of and exposed to many significant others. He learns to avoid "losing face" in front of others and to feel the shame of subtle ridicule, scorn, or outright ostracism from others. This propensity for feeling *hiya* attunes him to his insecurities and deficiencies. *Hiya* signifies embarrassment and inferiority more than the occasional sense of guilt and failure. For example, a Filipino may say, "I lost face because I was scolded in front of other people." This situation may trigger a violent reaction from the embarrassed person (for example, running amok). Other examples: "It is embarrassing to tell the doctor my true feelings"; "My family is ashamed of my sister's mental breakdown.")

Amor Propio

Great sensitivity to any personal affront that results in narcissistic wounding, particularly to lack of recognition of one's social status and family standing, is a prominent trait. There is a strong awareness of status. Socially prominent people, figures of authority, and the elderly expect and receive deference. Disregard of this expectation causes deep hurt to one's sense of self-regard, or *amor propio*.

Utang na Loob

In interpersonal relations this psychosocial concept refers to gratitude or reciprocal obligations and expectations based on favors or unsolicited services. Because of *utang na loob,* patients give gifts to their doctors and think twice before they file charges, even in the case of malpractice. Children's *utang na loob* with respect to their parents may force them to borrow money just to comply with the parents' request for financial support. The debt of gratitude may not have immediate payoffs, but it is expected to last forever—as long as the person with *utang na loob* is alive. Even that person's children and other relatives may continue to help pay back the favors. It is because of *utang na loob* that a Filipino remains in a job, even if it pays too little.

Crab Mentality

Personal ambition and the thirst for power may lead to the so-called *kanya-kanya* syndrome, characterized by selfishness, destructive competitiveness, and insensitivity to the interests of others, especially those outside one's clan. When colleagues have attained success and prestige, some Filipinos may react to them with the "crab mentality"—the tendency to put them down (as crabs in a basket pull each other down) with destructive criticism, backbiting, or gossip. The kinship system and regionalism contribute to this divisive tendency.

Bahala Na

This phrase refers to passive acceptance of one's fate, or to determination in the face of uncertainty. With their *bahala na* attitude, traditional Filipinos rarely avoid uncertain situations; instead they confront situations in spite of lacking information. This attitude may be a product of a social structure that motivates Filipinos to use their inherent resourcefulness, creativity, and courage to change problematic, unpredictable situations for the better. *Bahala na* may also mean "come what may." This sense of resignation helps Filipinos cope with the ill effects of events beyond their control. *Bahala* may also refer to being responsible or assuming the load. Accepting an uncontrollable situation, having faith in some higher power, and forging on with determination are the essence of this traditional value. The many natural disasters pummeling the Philippines, repeated colonizations, and political and economic devastation may all help create and encourage this particular value.

Lakas ng Loob

This socially admired trait has to do with inner resources for change, and with the courage to fight for freedom, justice, and dignity (Enriquez, 1990).

Pakikibaka

This term refers to uniting in a common struggle (Enriquez, 1990). It is the collective motivation to resist injustice and oppression.

Perseverance and Resilience

These traits are encouraged. As a people, the Filipinos have been likened to the bamboo, which sways and bends to the strong wind but bounces back after the storm. Indeed, they have survived many centuries of colonization and repeated natural disasters. Their ability to adapt to different situations and varying environments has already been noted.

Humility

Those who brag about their achievements or possessions are usually looked down on. Nevertheless, too much emphasis on humility may prevent Filipinos from being assertive about their abilities, skills, and talents, thus hindering well-deserved promotions. It is not uncommon for traditional Filipinos to disregard sincere appreciation and not acknowledge compliments, lest they give the impression of being too proud of themselves.

Hospitality and Generosity

In spite of limited resources, Filipinos help friends and relatives, and they welcome visitors with warmth and plenty of food. Health workers who visit patients' homes feel this hospitality, regardless of patients' social status.

Smooth Interpersonal Relationships and Social Acceptance

Filipinos stress the importance of being agreeable under difficult circumstances. Sensitivity to what other people feel at any given moment is very important. Euphemisms, humor, and teasing are all used to express bad feelings indirectly. Intermediaries are used to communicate and intercede during disagreements and when feelings are hurt.

Negative Effects of Some Cultural Traits

Immigration may precipitate, aggravate, or improve mental disorders. Some sociocultural factors may adversely affect the mental health of Filipino Americans (Araneta, 1982). For example, extreme personalism may impede the adjustment of Filipino Americans to an object- and task-oriented workplace. Because of personalism, Filipino American workers, even when qualified, may not assert themselves for promotions if they do not consider themselves personal friends of the boss or do not have personal connections in the personnel department. There may then be resentment of and hostility toward the person who is promoted, since he or she is perceived as being close to the supervisor.

Extreme family orientation creates an in-group attitude that prevents family members from expanding their social interactions. This impedes their acculturation and prevents them from establishing alternative social support in case the family disintegrates or the family members who provide the usual support are absent. Another effect of extreme family orientation is the tendency of the family to interfere too much in the personal affairs of its members (such as in the choice of a boyfriend or spouse). For example, a Filipino American family may force a daughter to marry someone perceived as a good provider who can help the family, instead of the boyfriend she really loves. After a few years, she divorces her husband because he wants to take her to another state, and she does not want to be separated from her family. In other cases, to have the feeling of belonging, people too used to having family support may be driven to join pseudofamilies, like gangs, when their own families break down. Excessive concern for the family's image and reputation may also prevent the timely treatment of family members with mental disorders. The family may refuse to ask for professional help because of the stigma associated with mental disorders and its effects on the prospects of the whole family.

Hiya, as a form of social control, may be so exaggerated that failures and disappointments have intense detrimental effects on self-esteem and lead to such mental problems as depression, suicide, and adjustment disorders.

The feeling of inferiority to Westerners, because of centuries of oppression and exploitation, may create passive, passive-aggressive, or dependent attitudes toward them. Too much deference to Westerners results in lack of initiative and assertiveness and impede economic and political mobility.

Because they try to get along with everyone, and because of the strong emphasis on interdependence, Filipino Americans have difficulties adjusting to the rugged individualism of American society. An identity crisis may become an important issue in mental health. The need to be agreeable in a group may also cause adolescent Filipino Americans to use drugs and alcohol and become involved in gang activities with their peers.

Conclusion

Filipino Americans tend to preserve their traditional family structure and dynamics as well as their common values and cultural traits. These traditions, values, and traits may help buffer the ill effects of migration but may also hinder the realization of the immigrants' goals and dreams in the United States.

Some sociocultural factors such as excessive personalism, extreme family orientation, overdeveloped sense of shame, colonial mentality, and immigration and legal problems affect the mental health of Filipino Americans in varying degrees.

Chapter 7

Belief Systems, Acculturation, and Mental Health Care

Immigrants must comfortably acculturate into their new country's health care system to most effectively utilize it. To make the mental health system in this country relevant to the recent and significant influx of Filipino immigrants, mental health care planners and clinicians must have a basic understanding of the kinds of mental health care sought and delivered in the Philippines at the present time and in the recent past. The immigrant's understanding of mental health care is significantly colored by his or her view of what causes mental illness and by his or her exposure to the Philippine mental health system, especially if he or she has been treated there.

As families petition for immigration on behalf of their siblings and parents, they bring in mental health patients as well, who may bring records and instructions in English from Philippines-based clinicians, as well as a few months' supply of Philippine-brand medications. For example, the Department of Immigration has a few requirements to enable a Filipino American family to welcome a mentally retarded brother from the Philippines. Their brother needs a Philippines-based mental health clinician (usually a psychologist or a psychiatrist) to state in writing that the brother has enough mental resources and adequate support in his new country to handle the process of immigration. A copy of his psychological test results may be included. In the United States, the family is required to search for a mental health clinician who will agree to evaluate the brother within several days of his arrival and make recommendations regarding his care or treatment, if needed. In evaluating the capacity of a mentally retarded Filipino immigrant, the clinician needs to take into account the vast extended-family system and the strength of interdependence mobilized for this obviously disabled member. In many rural Philippine settings, where having a mentally disabled family member is considered a portent of good luck, special treatment and gentle patience toward this member may be observed. In such a structured setting, he can be functional; in the new setting, his equilibrium may be disrupted, and he may become symptomatic. It is important to bear in mind that this is probably the very first time that the whole family has been exposed to any mental health clinician or to any formal mental health care, if recommended.

The new health care system must consider how a group of immigrants traditionally views the causes of illness (including mental illness). By the same token, the immigrants' access to and utilization of the new health care system and their response to preventive measures will be determined to some extent by their traditional views of illness. For example, Filipino Americans' attitudes toward AIDS will provide helpful clues to the kinds of educational materials that should be aimed at this particular population.

This chapter describes the state of mental health care and traditional attitudes toward illnesses in the Philippines. The experience in Shanghai, China, where the training of "foot doctors" was combined with the training of community-based teams in Western and indigenous healing practices, certainly points to the use of unique, culturally pertinent mental health programs that also take economics into account (Zhang, 1991). It must be emphasized that different countries have their own unique mental health systems. As a result, different immigrants to this country see their new country's mental health system from different points of view. For example, by contrast with their Filipino counterparts, present-day Korean immigrants have been exposed to a comprehensive, government-based medical insurance system since 1989. They have had access to more hospital beds and to more (and more varied) mental health clinicians. They have recently seen the mushrooming of quasi-medical enterprises and mental health facilities throughout their home country, enterprises such as stuttering-correction institutes, chiropractic clinics, and acupuncture clinics, all serving mentally ill patients (Kim, 1991; Rhi, 1989). Like their Filipino counterparts, present-day Korean immigrants have been exposed to Western psychiatric concepts through post–World War II American influence.

In the United States

By contrast with the Philippine mental health care system, the U.S. system has come a long way from hospital-based services. Care is given by a massive array of independent mental health practitioners—psychiatrists, psychologists, marital and family counselors, social workers, psychiatric nurses—working alone or with each other in clinics and groups. In the Philippines, mental health care is delivered by the traditional healers, psychiatrists, physicians, a few psychologists, and many clergymen and nuns. Other mental health professionals commonly work on hospital-based teams. Since patients can drop in to the family doctor's office and are seen on a first-come, first-served basis, many Filipino immigrants have no concept at all of keeping psychiatric appointments or even making appointments. This becomes a common reason for their dropping out of treatment, or for their being labeled "unmotivated," "uncooperative," or even "sociopathic" and "narcissistic" by their clinicians. Most important, the very concept of psychotherapy is alien unless the patient has undergone such treatment in the few big cities or in teaching hospitals in the native country. More commonly, the expectation in going to "the doctor's" office is to be given direct advice and medications for the body. Clinicians, regardless of their specialties, are often perceived in this light—a most perplexing if not frustrating experience for all the parties involved.

Even more confusing to the new immigrants are the health care insurance system, the emphasis on individuality and confidentiality, the relative barring of the extended family from actual treatment. Because there is no governmental health insurance in the Philippines, with the only recent emergence of a few private health insurance plans, immigrants from the rural Philippines may be more familiar with bargaining for their treatment fees and bringing gifts for the doctor.

The U.S. concern for individual civil rights is mirrored in legal decisions affecting mental health care (Lahen, 1984; Katz, 1989). The practice of psychiatry in the United States is regulated by state and federal laws, as well as by professional ethics. The nature of the therapeutic contract, informed consent, options for voluntary and involuntary hospitalization—these are relatively new concepts that have to be explained. The concept of confidentiality is another potential arena for frustration in the treatment of immigrants, whose identity may be strongly linked to interdependence within a vast extended-family network. The individual's confidentiality can still be protected, but the family should not be shut out, and family members should at least be listened to with respect and with recognition for their possibly intricate role in the patient's psychic struggles.

> **Vignette.** *A twenty-five-old single male was brought in by his grandfather for incipient psychotic depression. The "inquisitive" grandfather, who resided with the patient and his parents, was gently told that the evaluation session was highly confidential. His worried query—"What can I do to help?"—was answered with an appointment card for the next session. The grandfather and his grandson never came back, nor did they call to cancel the next session.*

In the Philippines

Many factors influence the present state of mental health care in the Philippines: the dire and plunging economic situation in the wake of political crises, the recent series of natural disasters (devastating earthquakes, typhoons, and volcanic eruptions), and the lack and maldistribution of mental health care staffing (Perlas and Buenaseda, 1991). Other factors are the predominantly indigenous treatment and understanding of mental illness, the unfamiliarity with psychiatry, the archipelago geography (with its effects on transportation and communication), the country's history of multiple colonizers, and the dominance of the Roman Catholic religion.

On a 1986 visit to the psychiatric unit of the regional hospital in Pototan, Iloilo, one of the present authors spoke to the staff and their patients about a pressing problem: lack of government money to keep the medicine supply constant. Reeling under years of the Marcos dictatorship, and the subsequent depletion of the treasury when the ruling political party fled the country, psychiatric units of regional hospitals housed and fed the patients, usually psychotic, in overcrowded quarters, with minimum budgets for food and shelter, and minimal hospital staffing. Both causing and compounding this lack of resources was the administrative structure of the government hospitals, which directly encouraged the neglect of psychiatric units. Regional hospital directors were themselves nonpsychiatrists, with no experience of mental hospitals. At times, psychiatric units were a considerable distance from the main hospitals (Perlas and Buenaseda, 1991).

With renewed attempts at democratization under the new political regime, and under the new chief of the Department of Health, who is knowledgeable about psychiatry, dramatic changes have occurred (Perlas and Buenaseda, 1991). A more thoughtful and systematic approach to mental health has been taken, with much input from local psychiatrists and the World Health Organization. Mental health care in the Philippines is still faced with many unique stumbling blocks, however, the most pressing one being the country's state of economic devastation. For example, there is still no systematic medical (much less psychiatric) insurance coverage for the nation's populace.

History

The history of psychiatry in the Philippines dates from the Western colonization of the country. Western concepts took root in the sixteenth century, with Spanish rule, and were succeeded in the nineteenth century by fifty formal years of American influence. The Spaniards started the movement that built psychiatric hospitals, still the central focus of public psychiatric care in the country. It was in the nineteenth century that some kind of psychiatric ward was established in the Hospicio de San Jose, in Manila; the first recorded patient was a Spanish sailor, and the ward catered to Spaniards. Another psychiatric ward was later established in the northern Philippines, at Cavite. This ward continued to house psychiatric patients during the American occupation. The government took an active interest and paid for hospitalizing patients from Manila, as well as a few from the provinces. Later still, a psychiatric unit was opened at the San Lazaro Hospital, in Manila, for patients from the provinces and, eventually, for all government-sponsored patients.

Under the Americans, the first city hospital was erected at San Juan del Monte, Rizal, in 1918. It was moved to Lolomboy, Bulacan, in 1921 and later to San Pedro, Makati, Rizal, in 1925. All these sites were in the vicinity of Manila, the capital city. On December 17, 1928, the Insular Psychopathic Hospital was opened to take in all the public psychiatric patients from the other hospitals. This hospital is now known as the National Center for Mental Health. It is the biggest psychiatric facility in the country, with branches on all the islands, and is run by the government for the general public (Sustento-Seneriches and Ladrido-Ignacio, 1983).

From the beginning, the psychiatric hospitals served mainly patients from Manila and the adjoining provinces. The rest of the islands were left with their indigenous ways of understanding and coping with mental disorders. Recognizing this deterrent to adequate nationwide mental health care, the Department of Health designated mental health coordinators for the fourteen regions. Each has its unique set of mental health problems and local resources. Lately, better follow-up care in the community, with more involvement from and education of patients' families, have resulted in decongestion of the public psychiatric wards. Special problem areas—mental retardation, epilepsy, drug abuse, and psychosocial disturbances in such special groups as overseas workers, street children, and victims of violence and disasters—have been recognized and included in planning (Perlas and Buenaseda, 1991).

In addition to the public mental health system just outlined, private general hospitals, as well as the teaching hospitals of the many medical schools in the big cities, have designated psychiatric rooms or wards. Outpatient clinics are likewise set up by some teaching hospitals, a few general hospitals, psychiatrists in private practice, and the Philippines Mental Health Association, in Manila (Sustento-Seneriches and Ladrido-Ignacio, 1983). By contrast with the situation in the U.S. and South Korean mental health systems, nonpsychiatric mental health professionals have not become a significantly autonomous faction of the caregiving community.

Other psychiatric facilities and services include rehabilitation centers for drug abusers; the Department of Public Health has just attached such centers to the regional hospitals. Patients who can afford to pay go to the "private wards" of some hospitals. A few private facilities, mostly in Manila, are available for patients with psychiatric illnesses and for mentally retarded patients. Special classes are sometimes offered in public schools for retarded pupils. Guidance counseling is offered in schools and colleges, and pastoral (including marital) counseling is widespread and well accepted in this predominantly Catholic setting, where advice for personal problems is sought from priests and nuns.

No known widespread statistical survey has been conducted, but it is common knowledge that Filipinos from all walks of life comfortably use both faith healers and physicians for behavioral symptoms, often at the same time. This is somewhat similar to the situation in Korea, where 66 percent of psychiatric outpatients have used multiple treatments (modern medicine, faith healing, and others), and where from 17 percent to 23 percent of psychiatric outpatients have been treated by shamans, 11 percent to 15 percent by faith healers, and 60 percent to 65 percent by traditional physicians (Lee, Hwang, and Yiu, 1973; Rhi, 1973). Even in their mental health practices, Filipinos show a facile blending of Eastern and Western concepts. Before the Spanish colonial era, there were indigenous explanations for and treatments of mental illnesses. Then came the concepts of Catholicism, with prayers, rituals, and exorcism. As of the early 1980s, about 120 psychiatrists were providing care along Western lines (Sustento-Seneriches and Ladrido-Ignacio, 1983). Other mental health clinicians work in hospital-based clinics in major cities; for all practical purposes, they are inaccessible to the majority of rural patients. As one result, the need for continued psychopharmacotherapy in the treatment of major psychiatric illnesses is frequently unmet because of the rural population's dire financial straits and lack of access to care. Unable to use the formal system of mental health care, and supported by old and familiar habits, these patients turn to their local healers and to the Church.

> Vignette. *The fifty-seven-year-old wife of a town counselor—an elementary school graduate and a housewife who had raised five children, including a medical student—sought treatment from the city psychiatrist for symptoms of a major depressive disorder, at the urging of her son. She was suicidal and had lost her appetite for food, sleep, sex, and all previous interests. She had crying spells and spent her time worrying about her health, concerned that her daughter-in-law had put a curse on her because of past misunderstandings. She was treated with antidepressants, individual psychotherapy, and family counseling. The local traditional healer performed concomitant rituals to rid her of the curse.*

> Vignette. *In a general hospital within a metropolitan area, a celled room was used for a young man who was withdrawing from multiple drug use and*

> *was suicidal. Medical treatment was given by a team comprising a psychiatrist, an internist, nurses, and a social worker. A unique feature was the use of a* bantay, *a person designated by the family to watch over the patient and minister to his needs, and even to help the nurses dispense medications.*

A bantay is also used by psychiatrists when they admit patients to a general hospital, usually during the acute phase of a mental illness (Sustento-Seneriches, 1984). For psychiatric patients, many general hospitals have designated barred rooms that can be locked, rather than staffed psychiatric wards.

> **Vignette.** *A Catholic priest intensively exorcised a psychotic adolescent. Weeks earlier, the adolescent's parents had paid a local healer to dance around him in a ritual, with offerings and incantations meant to appease and discourage fairies perceived as courting him to their way of life. When the symptoms quieted but then resumed, weeks later, the family brought the young man to the local doctor, who administered a commonly used and available phenothiazine. When the boy developed side effects and refused to take his medication, the family doctor sought consultation from a psychiatrist in a nearby city.*

Alternative mental health care programs using primary health care workers, nonphysician workers in the community, or primary health centers are being studied in conjunction with the World Health Organization (Ladrido-Ignacio and Tronco, 1991).

Beliefs About Causes of Illness

Beliefs are significant aspects of any culture. Traditional Filipino beliefs about the causes of illness are important to know so that health professionals can understand how Filipinos perceive and explain their illnesses, physical or mental, and can find alternative methods of intervention that are relevant and appropriate to the culture.

Generally, Filipinos do not classify their illnesses as either physical or mental; rather, they view them in a holistic manner, as having physical, psychological, mental, and spiritual components. Traditional Filipino theories or beliefs about the causes of illness are grouped into three categories: mystical, personalistic, and naturalistic (Tan, 1987). These categories are used mainly for organizing beliefs. In reality, Filipinos usually do not perceive a one-cause, one-effect pattern of causation. Instead, several factors are cited, closely interconnecting the categories. In the rural and urban Philippines, causes of illness have been perceived to be germs (73 percent), inadequacy or lack of nutritious food (66 percent), such natural elements as rain, cold, or wind (57 percent), God's will (15 percent), evil spirits (5 percent), and witchcraft (3 percent). Among Filipino Americans in Los Angeles, illnesses have been attributed to overeating, delayed eating, viruses, pollution, tension, body abuse, combining of incompatible foods, and divine punishment for sins.

Mystical Beliefs

Mystical beliefs about the causes of illness are assumed to be based on the concept that illness is a direct result of some experience or behavior of the victim. An example is the belief that God, the elders, or dead ancestors seek retribution, which results in illness and suffering.

> Vignette. *A retired Filipina nurse living in San Francisco had left her sick husband in the Philippines many years before and married in the United States, to change her visa status from tourist to permanent resident. She attributed the symptoms of her severe depression to* gaba *(divine or other supernatural retribution) because of her sins against her first husband and her arrogance toward her neighbors. To relieve her guilt and other symptoms, she went to*

> *church frequently, confessed her sins, and joined in prayer meetings. She also accepted treatment with antidepressants and was encouraged to continue her religious activities. With the support of her church and her religious friends, she felt better.*

Illnesses supposedly resulting from retribution are believed to be incurred through unfulfilled social obligations or actions that violate norms, such as incestuous marriage, disrespect of elders, and violence (Hart, 1979).

Another example of a mystical belief is the belief in soul loss. Some Filipinos believe that the soul can leave the body, especially when a person is sleeping, which results in illness. It is also believed that the soul has the "compulsion" to leave the body. There is a common belief in *bangungot,* a syndrome characterized by nightmares and sometimes by sudden death, commonly attributed to a heavy meal or to overeating before bedtime. When a "compulsive" soul wanders off, causing illness, this may also signify "compulsive tendencies" in persons who tend to deviate from society's norms (Tan, 1987). Common victims of *bangungot* are middle-aged males of low socioeconomic status. The belief in *bangungot* may be a form of social control that prevents people from overeating, especially before bedtime, but the syndrome may also be related to the existence of social pressures on and higher expectations for men, as well as to their inability to express feelings, especially when under stress (Tan, 1987). Thus the syndrome may be a representation of the danger of losing control of oneself, as expressed by patients who have experienced depersonalization.

Personalistic Beliefs

According to traditional personalistic beliefs, an illness is due to a supernatural being—a ghost, the soul of a dead person, an evil spirit, a witch, or a sorcerer (Tan, 1987). For instance, it is a common belief that severe mental disorders with bizarre symptoms are caused by *kulam* (sorcery). The *mangkukulam* (sorcerer), who may be hired by a jealous wife to harm her husband's mistress, uses incantations, prayers, voodoolike procedures, and poisons or sends a bad spirit to "abduct" the soul of the victim or to "possess" the victim. To counteract the *kulam,* the victim may hire another sorcerer believed to have stronger power, may request a priest to perform an exorcism, or may ask a faith healer to pray over the victim. One form of sorcery common in the Visayas is *barang,* which uses "pet" insects or animals to cause illness (Lieban, 1976). Environmental bad spirits, believed to live in mountains and trees and to be "not human," are also seen as causing illnesses.

> **Vignette.** *A Filipino husband living with his wife and children in San Francisco's Mission District (they had emigrated from a rural area in the Philippines about five years before) paid a Filipino spiritualist $200 to drive away an evil spirit in his house, believed to have caused his wife's chronic fatigue, insomnia, memory loss, irritability, and weight loss. The spiritualist performed the* orasyon *(a ritual using incantations, prayers, holy water, and religious articles) in the man's home. The family believed that the wife was being "played with" by the evil spirit. The patient was also brought to San Francisco General Hospital. She was diagnosed as having major depression and was treated with antidepressants.*

Witchcraft is also not uncommon among Filipinos. The witch is believed to have supernatural powers, such as the ability to fly or to transform himself or herself into something like a black cat or dog. Witches' common victims are believed to be pregnant women, babies, mistresses, and philandering husbands. To shield themselves from witches, *kulam,* and bad spirits, many Filipinos wear religious articles, such as crucifixes, rosaries, scapulars, medals, holy oils, or *anting-anting* (amulets). These articles may also be used as protection from accidents and illnesses and as aids in treatment of incurable illnesses.

Naturalistic Beliefs

According to naturalistic theories, the causes of illness are cold, winds, heat, thunder, and lightning, as well as diet, infection, humoral pathology, natural processes, and stress (Tan, 1987). "Fright illnesses," attributed to frightening experiences of thunder and lightning during childhood, are examples of the expression of naturalistic beliefs. In rural Cebu, the practice of *siging-siging,* a procedure whereby someone shakes the frightened person with both hands on the victim's shoulders while chanting, is used to minimize or drive away the person's fright or fear. This practice is also used with people who have had such frightening experiences as seeing a ghost or a dead person.

Disruption of the equilibrium of forces within the body is also believed to cause illness (for instance, through overexposure to cold or heat). *Pasma* (exposure illness) is believed to be due to exposure to cold at a time when the person is "hot" (during menstruation, after giving birth, or after prolonged physical activity), and vice versa. Filipino patients may refuse to drink cold water or juice with their medicine in the morning because they believe that cold drinks may upset their stomachs. Warm and humid air is believed to cause irritability and malaise.

Another cause of illness, according to naturalistic theories, is stress, which may be attributed to overexertion, prolonged hunger or thirst, debilitating extremes of hot and cold, worry, fear, or emotional disturbances. Stress is seen as the cause of such "modern" illnesses as heart problems, high blood pressure, migraine, anxiety disorders, and depression. Excessive worry is also believed to cause nervous breakdown, confusion, irritability, and malaise. Emotional stress due to frightening experiences is considered by the Visayans to be one of the causes of the *kabuhi* syndrome, characterized by frequent abdominal pain, dizziness, nausea, fatigue, anxiety, and other physical symptoms.

> **Vignette.** *A Filipina wife originally from Cebu consulted a Filipino physician for frequent stomachaches, headaches, ''being easily frightened,'' and ''nervousness.'' She told the doctor that she had*

> kabuhi *and characterized herself as* kabuhion *(a person prone to* kabuhi*). Upon further inquiry, she revealed that she was worried about her husband, who had not returned home from a gambling trip. She called her parents in Cebu and asked them to consult a* mananadna *(a person believed to have the power to locate lost persons and objects, as well as the ability to foresee events) in order to find her "lost" husband. The* mananadna *gave her parents specific instructions to find the woman's husband. The patient followed the instructions and found her husband in a northern California motel. Her* kabuhi *disappeared.*

Other natural and physical causes believed to cause illness include overeating, overwork, "oversex," a dirty environment, and genetic predisposition. The Filipino concept of heredity is that such diseases as mental illness, skin conditions, and tuberculosis are inherited, not through the chromosomes but through the blood. The notion of compatibility between drugs or food and the body is another important part of the Filipino belief system (Tan, 1987); incompatible foods and drugs may cause illness or ill effects. Therefore, patients may report to their doctors that they did not continue their medications because they felt that the medicine was not compatible with their diet or bodies. Many believe that certain families are susceptible to particular illnesses, such as mental illness and tuberculosis. These illnesses may be triggered by outside factors like stress, poor diet, prolonged hunger, and germs.

Implications

The U.S. mental health care system, backed up by research and studies, adheres mostly to theories of naturalistic disease causation. Since traditional Filipino beliefs also incorporate this concept, there is a need to underline this similarity through widespread, culturally sensitive education. However, the clinician must be acutely aware of the traditional holistic approach to causation and should ask about the presence of other beliefs that may affect the diagnosis and treatment of specific clinical problems. These beliefs are, after all, part of the Filipino client's psychic reality.

Traditional Beliefs and Acculturation

The degree to which Filipino Americans adhere to or implement traditional belief systems and outlooks on mental health care will vary according to several factors:

Degree of Acculturation to the Host Society

Acculturation and a social continuum existed among Filipino Americans even before their actual immigration to the United States. This continuum ranged from the most traditional, non-Westernized, rural, economically disadvantaged group to the sophisticated, Westernized, urban, affluent group (Araneta, 1982). Filipino immigrants who arrived during the first and second periods were considered the least acculturated and of low socioeconomic status, compared to more recent immigrants, who are predominantly professionals from urban areas and have been more exposed to Western values and life-styles (Marsella, Escudero, and Gordon, 1972). The acculturation process in general is influenced by age (older groups have slower acculturation and encounter more difficulties than younger ones), personality (which determines the coping response to change), attitude of the host community toward immigrants (discrimination and antiminority movements create hostility and resentment that impede acculturation), and similarities and differences between the native culture and that of the host country. The more similarities there are between the two cultures, the faster acculturation proceeds.

Length of Stay in the United States

Generally, the longer Filipinos reside in the United States, the less their tendency to preserve the traditional belief systems.

However, some Filipino Americans have been residing in the United States for decades yet continue to adhere closely to traditional beliefs and values.

Educational Level and Socioeconomic Status

Professionals and economically advantaged Filipino Americans are educated in a Westernized system even before they come to the United States. One should not assume, however, that a professional (such as a physician who comes from Manila) will no longer respond emotionally to perceived divine retribution or will no longer adhere to traditional family values. It is not uncommon even for professionals to consult folk or faith healers while seeing physicians for their own illnesses, especially for those considered incurable or bizarre (such as mental disorders).

Low-income and less educated Filipino Americans tend to adhere closely to traditional beliefs. At times, Filipino Americans may self-medicate, using substances from the Philippines (afraid that some U.S. medicines are too strong) and consulting folk healers, who usually do not charge fees. They may feel that folk or faith healers provide emotional, psychological, and spiritual healing and entail no problems from side effects or addiction (commonly feared with Western drugs).

Subethnic Groups and Community of Origin

Lowland Christian Filipino Americans, such as the Tagalogs and the Cebuanos, and those from urban communities may tend to adapt easily to Western values and life-styles by comparison with Muslim Filipino Americans and those from rural areas. Muslims, constituting 6 percent of the Filipino population, will likely resist Western values just as they successfully resisted the Spanish and American colonizers.

Generational Level

First-generation Filipino Americans tend to continue adhering to the Filipino belief systems. They manifest the basic cultural characteristics more than the second and succeeding generations do.

Location and Type of Residence in the United States

Filipino Americans residing in cities with multicultural groups, like San Francisco and New York, tend to have faster acculturation than those living in ethnic enclaves, unicultural communities, and rural areas. Multiethnic societies are also more tolerant of adherence to traditional values and belief systems, which minimizes the stress of trying to adapt to a new culture and prevents higher risk for mental disorders. Bicultural orientation is also facilitated in these settings. Ethnic enclaves or ghettos do provide a supportive and ethnocentric environment for the new immigrants, but prolonged residence in this type of community impedes faster acculturation to the socioeconomic and political mainstream.

Conclusion

The differences between the mental health care systems of the United States and the Philippines are substantial. Immigrants must understand the U.S. system in order to effectively use it.

Key to treating the mentally ill Filipino American is an understanding of how immigrants view the cause of illness. Adherence to the traditional Filipino beliefs on the causation of illness vary according to factors such as degree of acculturation to the host country, length of stay in the United States, age of arrival in the United States, and so on.

Chapter 8

Guidelines for Assessing Filipino American Clients

There is a dearth of materials on cross-cultural assessment concerning Filipino American patients. Conveniently, yet unjustifiably, this population is usually lumped together with the rest of the Asian American groups and given a global Asian label. But the Asian populations studied most have been Chinese, Japanese, and, lately, Vietnamese (Arkoff, Thaver, and Elkind, 1966; Leong, 1986). As a result, Filipino Americans are stereotyped as Asians in the psychiatric literature. Articles on actual clinical assessment of and therapy with Filipino American patients are relatively rare and sparsely written (Leong, 1986; Anderson, 1983).

This chapter compiles relevant and available materials and contributes our observations and experiences in practice, and, more important, encourages readers to recognize the blatant gap in knowledge. We hope in this way to spur further discussion, writing, and research on Filipino Americans' mental health.

Goals of Cross-Cultural Assessment

Thorough cross-cultural clinical assessment is mandatory for accurate diagnosis and for appropriate treatment and intervention in the context of the patient's culture. The first requirement is to collect descriptive information on the presenting symptom(s) or problem(s), in order to arrive at a working diagnosis or clinical impression. This information will then serve as a guide to treatment and further intervention. A second goal is to collect data on the chronological events of the patient's life that have led to the present problem. It is also important to gather information on how the patient and the family conceptualize and categorize the illness, its causes, its precipitants, its contributory factors, and the perceived best treatment and best person to treat the illness.

Sociocultural factors that facilitate or hinder treatment must be reviewed. Beliefs and fears about the effects of mental illness on the patient and the family should also be assessed, as should effects on the patient's job opportunities, relationships, social standing, and legal and immigration status. For example, a Filipino patient may refuse to be treated by a psychiatrist for clinical depression because he is afraid of having "mental records" that will prevent his getting a good job, and because of a possible increase in his medical insurance premium. He may request to be treated "without medical records," if treatments are necessary.

The Patient

To understand and fully use the initial interview process, the clinician must consider several factors within the patient and within the patient's significant relationships. First, the reasons why the patient has come to the clinician must be understood and seen in light of the fact that unacculturated Filipino Americans tend to shy away from consulting doctors for psychological problems. The question "Why now?" must be explored in the context of the patient's and the family's conceptualization of the illness, with respect to sociocultural factors. The clinician must be curious about these reasons, as well as about recent changes in attitude on the part of the patient and the family or on the part of friends who accompany the patient. Were there blatantly disruptive or culturally dystonic behaviors in the patient, forcing the family to seek help? Did a respected friend or priest convince the patient to seek help? Did a respected family doctor or pediatrician refer the patient?

> Vignette. *A twenty-five-year-old unmarried Filipino American was brought in to the psychiatric emergency clinic by the police because he was threatening to harm his mother. Unemployed for almost a year after having been fired from his job, he had been allowed to stay home and not work. He told his family that he had been discriminated against in his workplace and now needed some rest. Because he was the only child of working parents who were all too sympathetic about his alleged job discrimination, he rarely went out, and he slept a lot.*
>
> *There was denial and ignorance in the parents' part about a possible mental illness. They tolerated his "laziness," rationalizing that he "only wanted some time out." When the father had a stroke, however, the mother started to nag her son about looking for a job. The son became more reclusive and told his mother that he had seen the spirits of his deceased grandparents.*
>
> *A faith healer conducted several "laying on of hands" sessions, which calmed the son and comforted the mother. Soon, however, the son became more withdrawn and agitated. During one of his mother's verbal confrontations, he shouted that he wanted to kill her. He was later found in church, walking on his knees toward the altar, a knife in his hand, at which point he was brought to the clinic.*
>
> *The parents had not considered his dependence, excessive sleeping, and withdrawal abnormal, and so they had not asked for help. Only the father's illness caused the mother to confront her son, which triggered conflict and manifestations of psychiatric symptoms. The faith healing delayed psychiatric treatment, but when the symptoms became severe and life-threatening, psychiatric treatment became the last recourse, as often happens.*

Second, any delineated motive or purpose for the consultation must be determined. Did the patient come in for a doctor's certificate because work was missed for a week? Did the patient come in for a few days' supply of sleeping medications? Did the patient come to placate a spouse, or because of a court order following allegations of child abuse?

Third, it is quite helpful to know the person or persons who were influential in encouraging the patient to seek help. These may be the people who accompany the patient to the first interview. These may also be the people who become involved during the patient's eventual treatment. The clinician must bear in mind that interdependence, rather than autonomy, is the norm in the traditional Filipino American family.

Fourth, the patient's and the family's expectations about the assessment must be understood. The concept of a psychiatric interview is foreign to the traditional Filipino American patient. Psychiatry is a relatively new specialty in the Philippine setting, and direct advice is usually expected from doctors. Medications are also expected to give immediate results. The patient may focus on somatic symptoms and may expect advice on diet and life habits believed to affect health.

Using the medical model as the point of entry to clinical assessment is beneficial to Filipino Americans and to other Asian patients, who may feel stigmatized or uncomfortable if they perceive themselves as having psychiatric problems. Because many of them seek help for their physical symptoms rather than for emotional distress, it is culturally congruent to evaluate their symptoms within a medical model that assumes the possibility of organic causes. Therefore, the clinician should inquire about the patient's symptoms, searching for medical causes before openly exploring the patient's psychological distress and conflicts; by then, the physician will have gained the patient's confidence. If a Filipino patient refers symptoms or pain to particular parts of the body, he usually expects the physician to examine those areas, in typical settings and with standard procedures. It is not uncommon for a relative or a friend to accompany the patient, who may even request that person to be present during the physical examination (except a gynecological examination) or initial assessment. If the patient is fearful about the examination or assessment, especially during the first visit, the accompanying person's presence can allay this fear. Valuable information may be elicited from or shared by this person, which will help in the assessment and in the subsequent plan for intervention. If the physical symptoms need further evaluation with laboratory procedures, the reasons should be explained carefully. If fears based on traditional beliefs are listened to, then appropriate reassurances can be offered.

> **Vignette.** *A fifty-seven-year-old Filipina from a rural area of her native country prided herself on her ability to work in the local hotel and thereby contribute to the family's finances. She became depressed when an accident at work injured her shoulder. She was referred to the psychiatrist because her orthopedist and her physical therapist suspected an underlying psychosis when her physical symptoms became worse and she asked "inappropriate" and frightened questions about physical therapy.*
>
> *She became highly cooperative when the psychiatrist offered to help her communicate with her orthopedist, her physical therapist, and even her employer about her symptoms, her adjustment to the shoulder problems, and her desire to go back to work. She was hurt that "they think I am malingering." Her fears about treatment concerned heat and cold therapies, which she viewed as highly uncomfortable if not potentially destructive to her body, according to her traditional understanding of the necessary balance between heat and cold. The psychiatrist acknowledged her traditional concepts and discussed the diagnostic and therapeutic procedures. The psychiatrist immediately became a trusted authority figure, who could explain Western medicine to her and reassure her fears. She was then able to share some depressive thoughts and feelings about her injury.*

Physicians are familiar authority figures in the Philippines. If the clinician is perceived as an authority figure, then the Filipino patient will readily cooperate during assessment. Preferably, the physician (including a psychiatrist) will initiate the assessment before other mental health professionals (psychologists and social workers) evaluate the patient. Psychiatrists are perceived as physicians before they are considered psychiatrists (a term that Filipino Americans commonly associate with "mental" or "crazy" patients only). As patients become more comfortable and trust the physician as someone who can help with their problems, they will not feel stigmatized even when they learn that the physician is a psychiatrist.

In outpatient medical clinics, where many Filipino Americans seek help for all their health needs, including mental health, the primary physician is the preferred person for initiating an assessment. However, the physician should also be trained to detect psychological symptoms that accompany physical symptoms, so that he or she can refer patients with psychiatric problems to appropriate mental health professionals for further evaluation. The chances that the patient will accept psychiatric or psychological evaluation are higher if the trusted primary physician recommends it and explains why the referral is necessary but refrains from labeling the referral as a "mental evaluation." The word *mental* generally has a negative connotation among Filipino Americans.

> **Vignette.** *At a health fair in Daly City, considered the "Manila of California," since more than one-third of the population is Filipino American, a group of Filipino American mental health professionals put up a sign reading* MENTAL HEALTH *in a booth and prepared to distribute brochures and other information about their services. Very few Filipino Americans visited the booth until a perceptive Filipino American psychiatrist removed the sign, put out his blood-pressure apparatus and stethoscope, and announced that he was willing to take the blood pressure of anybody who visited the booth. Within just*

a few minutes, many Filipinos had visited the booth. After taking their blood pressure, the physician-psychiatrist gave them brochures and information about available health services, which included mental health services.

Finally, Filipino Americans' past experiences with and biases about the U.S. culture and health system may influence their expectations. Expectations are further influenced by degree of acculturation, which in turn affects understanding of American mental health concepts and comfort with the American mental health system.

Blending of Concepts

Many times, the patient's orientation to mental health, illness, and treatments represents a blend of traditional Filipino concepts, in varying proportions. Does the patient adhere to the heat-and-cold (*pasma*) causation of anxiety symptoms and expect concrete advice from the therapist along these lines? Does the patient expect the clinician to have a couch or dramatically perform hypnosis, as in Hollywood presentations of psychotherapy?

Vignette. *A thirty-year-old first-generation Filipino American sought the help of a psychiatrist for restless insomnia lasting a month. As soon as he came into the office, he went to the sofa, took off his shoes, laid down, and told the psychiatrist that he was ready for hypnosis. He was wearing a scapular, and later he talked about saying a novena for the intercession of certain saints regarding his problems. He reported the use of herbs to help him sleep. The assessing clinician had to acknowledge all these attempts at self-treatment as he formulated his assessment.*

The more acculturated the Filipino American psychiatric patient is, the closer his or her expectations of the assessment hour will be to those of American patients. Thus an acculturated third-generation Filipino American couple will seek out a child psychiatrist without hesitation for their son who manifests school phobia.

The Clinician

Clinicians must be aware of their biases, theoretical leanings, and expectations during the initial assessment hour. They may need to devise systems (a family system, for example) or a bioneurochemical or psychodynamic diagnosis immediately after the assessment, and their questions may be directed toward this goal. Their ability to listen to the patient's presented materials may also be geared to making the diagnosis along a certain line of theory.

Is there a traditional tendency for the therapist to be passive? Is he or she more interactive? Clinicians may have preconceived notions, and studies have shown the presence of cultural biases in clinicians during the assessment of Asian American patients (Leong, 1986). Although this issue has not been studied specifically with Filipino Americans, cultural stereotyping has been demonstrated in clinicians dealing with some Asian groups and lower-class minority groups.

The clinician's fund of knowledge about the Filipino culture, and the traditional Filipino orientation to mental health, illness, and treatment, will play a considerable role in the assessment of the patient. The clinician must be aware of behaviors that fall within the norm of the Filipino American who passes through the different stages of acculturation. For example, a Western orientation would frown on the traditional Filipino American patient's tendency to defer all financial savings toward the children's college education, to the detriment of his or her own retirement.

> **Vignette.** *A Filipino American widow who consulted a Caucasian clinician had physical symptoms obviously related to her problematic relationship with a daughter in college, who had a new boyfriend. The clinician's questions centered on the mother's finan-*

cial support of the daughter, who was not encouraged to find work but to devote her time to her studies (thus the obvious interdependence). This is a cultural norm: the parent provides the best education for the daughter, who is then expected to help her mother in the mother's old age. The mother and the daughter had no problem with this expectation, but they were having differences regarding the daughter's dating habits.

If clinicians are Western in their values and traits, then their value systems may veer toward a Western orientation, and they may minimize, disregard, overlook, or fail to recognize traditional Filipino American cultural values.

Cultural Presentations of Symptoms

There are indications that actual symptoms are culturally colored. For example, brief psychosis has been described in Filipino patients, and the same types of cases have also been noted among Filipino American patients. Psychotic ideations of schizophrenic patients have been differentiated between Filipino American and Japanese groups in Hawaii. The tendency to somatize symptoms has also been noted among depressed Filipino American patients. There are indeed culture-bound syndromes found predominantly among Filipinos.

Language Barrier

Although English is the second language of the Philippines, numerous factors continue to produce very real communication problems between new immigrants and clinicians. Many new Filipino immigrants have heavy accents, are elderly, or are from remote rural areas and cannot communicate in English. Moreover, there are 111 dialects and many subcultures in the Philippine archipelago. Even if clinicians are Filipino, they may not speak their patients' dialects.

If Filipino American patients have immigrated during

later childhood, they will carry the original Filipino accent. According to the regions they came from, they may transpose *p*'s and *f*'s and will have difficulty pronouncing *e, a, i,* and *o.* At times, Filipinos may interchange *he* and *she* when speaking English because there is only one pronoun, *siya* to denote both genders in the Filipino language. Often there is no English translation for many symptoms and descriptions of feelings. For example, a Filipino patient who complains of frequent headaches may also reveal that his head "becomes hot easily"—a literal translation of *mainit ang ulo,* which means "I am easily angered." The physician may then request a nurse to take the patient's temperature, in order to rule out fever.

Interpreters or translators may adversely affect an assessment. The translator may be another Filipino but may not be able to understand, much less accurately interpret, what the patient is trying to say if the patient uses an unfamiliar dialect and cannot speak in Philipino or English. Moreover, the Filipino translator is subject to his own countertransferential view of the patient's familiar world. A trained Filipino interpreter is still the ideal person to assist the clinician who does not understand the patient's primary language, but reality does not allow this "luxury" in most medical and psychiatric settings. If a translator is not available, the clinic should defer making a final diagnosis until further exploration and evaluation, preferably with a Filipino clinician or a culturally trained clinician.

Cultural Traits and Values Affecting Communication

There is a high degree of personalism in the unacculturated Filipino American's mode of relating to others. There is hesitancy about going to an unfamiliar clinic or office unless it is known to the patient or recommended by somebody close to or familiar with the patient. Thus there is usually a "*padrino* (patron) system" for the initial assessment. The patient may even arrive with the person who is a known entity to the clinic or the clinician. The *padrino* may be another patient, a friend or relative of a staff member, or the referring doctor or priest who has worked within the system. Introductory or exploratory phone calls may well precede the first assessment hour.

This is the same trait that will propel the patient and the family to expect the clinician to wait for them when they arrive late, or to extend the assessment hour if the process is not explained to them. The clinician may even be invited to perform the assessment in the patient's home, or on a day or at a time most convenient for the patient.

> **Vignette.** *A first-generation Filipino American from the rural Philippines sought the help of a Filipino American psychiatrist. He had been seen in a busy facility by a non-Filipino psychiatrist who "kept on canceling my appointments." Expecting the doctor to understand his difficulties in using public transportation, the patient saw nothing wrong with arriving fifteen minutes late for appointments, and he felt personally rejected when his appointments were canceled. His doctors in the rural Philippines had worked in walk-in clinics, with no formal appointments. The patient felt ashamed to discuss his feelings with the first psychiatrist, and he did not show up for his last appointment.*

The office procedures should have been explained to this patient, with emphasis on every patient's (not just his) need to arrive on time. During the initial assessment hour, shows of informality and expectations of special treatment (especially if a *padrino* has initiated the consultation) must be dealt with patiently and firmly.

The tendency toward personalism is also behind the patient's and the family's unembarrassed way of asking the clinician personal questions: "Are you married?" "Do you live in the area?" "How many children do you have?" These questions are not necessarily indications of instant transference; they are the traditional Filipino way of bridging the unfamiliarity of a situation. They can also start the process of incorporating the clinician into the family's hierarchy system, where he or she usually will be seen as a respected authority figure. Gifts may be given to the clinician for the same reason.

If the clinician is Caucasian, the patient and the family may well regard him or her through a "colonial mentality"—

that is, with feelings of inferiority. The patient may then hesitate to share what are deemed to be embarrassing data, which will make the clinician look down on him. There may be diffidence, shyness, and hesitancy to question the clinician's suggestions, even if the patient does not agree with the clinician.

Another traditional Filipino trait is the propensity to maintain smooth interpersonal relationships. There may be hesitancy to say no directly, and euphemisms or circumlocution may be used.

If the clinician is used to the Western way of communicating directly and reporting feelings as they are, the traditional Filipino way of relating can be frustrating and hard to comprehend. In our experience, traditional Filipino Americans, who retain the Spanish influence, tend to be more expressive of their emotions than other Asian groups. Nevertheless, Asian Americans have been observed to have a "lower level of verbal and emotional expressiveness than do whites" (Leong, 1986). Other factors—such as respect for authority and elders, the colonial mentality, and the need for smooth interpersonal relationships—can make the Filipino American patient appear passive or reticent to the Western clinician. Therefore, degree of acculturation, level of education, and the region of the Philippines that the patient comes from will also affect his or her nonverbal communication.

Conclusion

Cross-cultural assessment of Filipino Americans is a requirement for accurate diagnosis and for planning culturally sensitive interventions. The guidelines presented in this chapter provide an overview of the factors critical in assessing Filipino Americans. Critical information such as the patient's and family's conceptualization of the causes, treatment, and precipitants of the illness; their perceived best treatment; their fears; and their sociocultural history before, during, and after immigration help the mental health service provider plan the most appropriate interventions.

Chapter 9

Treatments and Interventions

Given the paucity of literature on cultural considerations in treatment, we will share our experiences in treating Filipino American clients. Because most Filipino Americans are first-generation immigrants, our discussion will be primarily about this group. Chapter Eight delineated the bases on which patients should be individually evaluated. This chapter discusses cultural factors that are predominant among Filipino American patients. The patient's personal and family history should also be considered, however, and caution must be exercised with respect to overgeneralizing.

Cultural Considerations in the Psychotherapy of Depressed Filipino American Patients

A review of the records of the South of Market Mental Health Clinic, situated in an area heavily populated with Filipinos, shows that of the 305 cases seen from January 1987 to April 1988, only 21 were Filipinos, and only 11 were given a diagnosis of major depression, dysthymic disorder, or adjustment disorder with depressive features. Observably, depressed Filipinos are not seeking the care they need from the local mental health clinic, given that the prevalence rate of clinical depression in the Filipino community is 27.3 percent. Part of the reason is that most Filipinos still are not familiar with the services provided by a mental health clinic. They also equate the need to go to a mental health clinic with being "crazy" (a source of shame). Some also feel that they would rather not go to a professional and pay a fee when they could tell their friends about their problems for free. This situation is unfortunate because by the time these patients come to the attention of a mental health professional, their condition is already so severe that they are either psychotically depressed or suicidal. Nevertheless, once these clients have entered a mental health clinic, relevant cultural factors must be included, both in making a diagnosis and in formulating treatment plans.

Diagnosis

Most Filipinos can understand and speak English, but using the native language to express emotions is still most comfortable for them. Tagalog is the principal native language, but patients under stress may revert to one of about 111 dialects (Ignacio, 1991). The interpreter must be able to explain not only verbal but possibly also any culturally determined nonverbal behavior. It is not enough to ask, "Are you feeling sad or depressed?" Questions that would correlate with Filipinos' conceptual experience of depression should also be asked, so that depression can be identified correctly: "What bothers you a lot?" "What kinds of problems have you been experiencing?" These questions are more meaningful.

Treatment

Filipinos' concepts of Western medical care are closely linked with their ideas about prescription medications. They expect that when they go to a doctor, they will be given pills to treat their ailments. This is not unlike their expectation of traditional folk healers, who dispense medicinal herbs and potions. Even if a medication has only a placebo effect, a prescription for it ensures that the patient will stay in treatment. We have sometimes prescribed antidepressants in subtherapeutic doses, with patients describing "magical" results.

Psychotherapy is not a form of treatment that Filipinos are accustomed to, however. Clinicians must not take the classic passive stance. Rather, they should be active in making connections with their clients' thoughts, emotions, feelings, and physical complaints. It is equally important to consider some Filipino cultural traits. For example, shame (*hiya*) is a strong operational factor in the psychological world of the Filipino. The following vignette illustrates how it may lead to therapeutic failure if not sufficiently addressed.

> **Vignette.** *An elderly depressed Filipino was referred because he was having problems concentrating on his job. He had left a lucrative medical practice in the Philippines, only to find that he could not pass the U.S. licensing exam and could work only as a laboratory technician. The psychiatrist naively began to explore feelings about loss of status, thinking that this was the cause of the depression, without acknowledging the patient's shame at coming to see an upstart Filipino American doctor who obviously had made it in the United States, while he himself was a failure. Although the psychiatrist thought that he had made a very good connection during the first session, the patient never came back.*

Perhaps it would have been better if a nonmedical therapist had seen this patient instead. The feeling of shame can be so strong that it may become the major focus of therapy.

> **Vignette.** *A fifty-eight-year-old man was referred because of sleep problems. An internist had prescribed various sleep medications, with no significant improvement. In therapy, the patient revealed that he had come to the United States in 1972, as a tourist, and decided to stay permanently. In 1974, he had*

found someone who gave him a well-paying job and sponsored him for a visa. He had been able to send money home and had also been saving some, so that he could send for his wife and three children.

His boss died suddenly in 1975. He was not able to find a permanent job after that, and he started to worry so much that he developed a peptic ulcer, for which he was hospitalized in 1977. In 1983, he was still unemployed and staying with friends, who occasionally gave him some money for doing menial jobs. Although he had been through several years of struggle, he was adamant about not returning to the Philippines. He admitted missing his family, but he thought that he probably would not recognize his children because they were now grown. Moreover, he was ashamed at not having fulfilled his promise to bring them to the United States.

With antidepressant medication, his sleep became normal. The psychotherapist pointed out to him that his chances of getting a good job were very small, because of his age and because he was essentially unskilled, and that he might be better off in the Philippines, where at least he had more family support. It took nearly three years before he accepted that fact, and only after the therapist repeatedly told him that he could use the excuse that he had become ill and could not work, and so there was nothing to be ashamed about.

Vignette. *A fifty-seven-year-old man was referred after he was hospitalized for suicidal ideation and vegetative symptoms of depression. He had become depressed when a new manager at work gave him a poor job-performance evaluation. Initially, the therapist thought that the patient had become depressed because of the threat of losing his job after the poor evaluation. But further exploration re-*

> *vealed that the evaluation was a source of shame to him, because for several years he had been someone whom everyone in his office looked up to. In therapy, it became clear to him that he was just one of the victims of the new manager's form of harassment, and that there really was no reason for him to be ashamed. He filed a suit against the company, and his lawyer assured him that he had a strong case. His depression vanished.*

Another cultural factor that may affect treatment is *utang na loob,* the deep feeling of gratitude and sense of reciprocity about favors. In its positive aspect, it may be conveyed by patients who bring gifts to their therapists, especially at Christmas. Negatively, it may be used by parents to make their children accountable, since the ultimate *utang na loob* concerns the child's indebtedness to the parents for giving life.

> Vignette. *A twenty-year-old Filipina was referred after taking an overdose of pills. She felt distressed because she could not adjust to life in the United States, and she resented the fact that she had to work part-time while attending college classes because her mother could not afford to support her with her own meager income. She could not tell her mother that she wanted to go back to the Philippines, because she felt that her mother wanted her here and needed her help—at the expense of the patient's leading a miserable life.*
>
> *The therapeutic work centered on seeing the patient and her mother together, helping the patient express her feelings, and making the mother realize that the patient could get her college degree faster in the Philippines, so that if she chose to come back, she could find a better job. The patient later wrote from the Philippines, saying that she was happy and doing well in school, and that she wrote to her mother regularly, assuring her that everything was all right.*

The Filipino's tendency to suppress emotions in order to maintain smooth interpersonal relationships may eventually contribute to the development of a depressive disorder.

> **Vignette.** *A fifty-four-year-old Filipina was referred from the medical clinic because of various somatic complaints. She was assessed to be clinically depressed. Her husband had died suddenly of a heart attack three years before, and she had not been able to mourn his death. She had been very dependent on him, but she also had silently suffered his many infidelities. She stated she had stayed in the marriage only because of her religion, and because her mother had suffered the same fate with her father. She also resented the fact that her five children had not given her the same respect that they had given their father. In therapy, she was encouraged to ventilate her anger toward her husband, to be more assertive with her children, to reclaim her role as a parent, and to establish her independence. By the time therapy had terminated, she was learning how to drive.*

A word about immigration: In the last few years, as mentioned before, a wave of immigrants has been given the pejorative name TNT (*tago ng tago,* or "hiding and hiding"). The modus operandi is to come to the United States on a tourist visa and then try to stay permanently, by entering into an arranged marriage with a U.S. citizen or someone else with a permanent visa. If the immigrant is already married, a divorce is mutually agreed upon by the couple, with the understanding that they will remarry after a visa is obtained, and after a divorce from the person who helped obtain the visa. The complications and disruptions to family life resulting from such an arrangement can be imagined.

> **Vignette.** *A thirty-five-year-old woman tried to scare her husband by drinking bleach. In 1982, she and*

her husband had come as tourists. After four months, they decided to get a divorce so that the husband could marry a Filipina who already had a visa.

The wife went back to their two sons in the Philippines. After a year, she returned. She found herself sharing an apartment with her husband's new "wife." Gradually, she became more and more jealous and suspected her husband of sleeping with the other woman. Her suicidal attempt was her way of telling her husband that she could no longer be in the same house with the other woman. In therapy, the couple redefined the original purpose of their arrangement and their desire to continue working toward their goal. They eventually moved to a separate apartment, risking the possibility that immigration authorities would discover them.

In summary, when a depressed Filipino patient is seen in therapy, cultural traits that may be affecting the patient's condition should be considered, in addition to the usual dynamic formulations of the causes of depression. The success or failure of treatment may depend on attention to such cultural factors.

Family Involvement

Because of the primacy of the family, it is almost impossible to embark on any form of psychotherapy with a Filipino client without an understanding of the client's family or clan situation and an appreciation of interdependence as a cultural norm among extended-family members. Members of the nuclear family, the extended family, family friends, and personal friends may intrude into the therapy format at almost any stage and should be carefully evaluated and considered for their actual and varied involvement in the therapeutic process. One complaint of the staff at a psychiatric day care program was that the parents of two Filipino patients sat on the doorstep all day. The staff viewed this as irregular, intrusive, and disruptive. They did not speak to the parents about the parents' need to be close to their family members, much less involve them in the program. By sharp contrast, a family representative, or *bantay,* is an integral part of the inpatient psychiatric milieu in Philippine general hospitals (Sustento-Seneriches, 1984): cottages in a rehabilitation program planned for chronic psychiatric patients at the old National Mental Hospital in the Philippines included facilities for the patient's family.

> **Vignette.** *A professor from the Philippines, visiting his sister, set up an appointment for himself in a psychiatrist's office. He brought his sister and the sister's young son with him. The nephew, in the acute phase of a paranoid disorder, was the real patient. The visiting uncle, concerned for his nephew's welfare, brought him for treatment in a roundabout way.*

Given the traditional interdependence among Filipino family members, it is not unusual for one respected, designated, or key member to speak for the whole family, or to intervene directly for the sake of the family's welfare. A common reason why some Filipinos change therapists is because the first therapist speaks directly only to the patient and disregards the family's queries about or interest in the therapy. In dealing with an adolescent or a second-generation patient, the patient's need to adjust to an autonomy-centered culture must be finely balanced with his or her ongoing relationship with a family where interdependence is the norm. The therapist must carefully decide when to exclude family members from the therapy format and when to include them, maintaining a healthy respect for both cultural norms. Confidentiality issues must also be discussed, as appropriate.

Family Hierarchy

A well-recognized hierarchy system exists in the Filipino family, according to seniority: the grandparents, followed by the parents, and then by the children, in descending order by age. Filipino families commonly migrate piecemeal to the United

States, but there is a concerted effort to bring the entire family into the country. It is not unusual for all three generations to live together.

Often, in-laws and other members of the extended family live under one roof. In such a setting, roles are designated or eventually developed within the household. The therapist must understand these family roles in order to formulate the patient's psychodynamics within the family system and plan family-oriented intervention, if necessary. Knowing who is the most influential "elder" within the family structure can be helpful to the therapist in the beginning phase of treatment (which Kim, 1992, also recognizes as an important but rocky engagement process with his Korean-American patients). Patients who are unfamiliar with and dubious of the mental health system may be inclined to cancel or not show up for appointments. Harnessing the cooperation of influential family members can go a long way toward persuading patients to try therapy, if only out of respect for these family members. The family influence may also be felt across the Pacific.

> **Vignette.** *A recent immigrant, a woman in her sixties, had a hard time giving up her role as the respected elder for her extended family in the Philippines. She was deluged with phone calls and letters from "home," and she felt guilty and depressed in the comparative isolation of her U.S.-based family. The therapist found it useful to involve significant family members in the Philippines by phone, and to discuss their letters in therapy.*

Therapists should note who accompanies patients to their appointments, or who shows up during visiting hours at the hospital. It is not unusual for all three generations to be present at some point, if family therapy is conducted. Because of the high regard for authority, children or younger siblings may be deterred from speaking their innermost thoughts about their "elders" during therapy. Parents and grandparents may be oversensitive to any show of disrespect by the children, or they may be protected by the rest of the family from losing face. Euphemisms, jokes, and anecdotes are often used to soften the impact of messages. The therapist who is sensitive to these dynamics can consider several combinations of interventions during family therapy. The parents can be seen alone, without the children, for some strategic sessions. The children and the parents can likewise be seen without the grandparents.

The role of mediator is an acceptable one within such a hierarchical system, and any family member may play this role at any given time in the service of family harmony. The therapist may be called upon to mediate in specific circumstances. A common transference phenomenon is for the family to see the therapist as a respected elder, an older sibling, or a parent. He or she is easily incorporated into the family hierarchy system and is looked up to for direct advice. In such a situation, a passive stance on the part of the therapist would be incomprehensible, especially in the early phases of therapy. Behavior-modification strategies can be devised with certain members, who can be instructed to follow through on new behaviors toward the patient, as long as these family members understand how these changes will help the patient.

Countertransference

The clinician's attitudes toward and biases regarding Filipino Americans or other Asians can lead to a variety of countertransference issues. In a Filipino American therapist, common countertransference phenomena are overidentification with the patient and the patient's family, denial of painful acculturation issues common to both patient and therapist, and boundary problems.

Psychopharmacotherapy

The use of chemicals for relief of emotional distress, including depression, has been incorporated into the herbalist's practice in the Philippines (Tan, 1987; Sustento-Seneriches, 1984). Even indigenous healers in the Philippines and in the United States refer patients to psychiatrists "for medications." Since the 1950s, psychopharmacotherapy has become an integral (if not a forefront) component of psychiatric care in the Philippines as well.

Since the 1950s, there have been reports and sharings of clinical vignettes indicating that Asian patients respond to much lower doses of psychotropics (and, indeed, develop side effects at lower doses) than do their Caucasian counterparts (Lin and Poland, 1989). In the 1980s, results of well-designed studies began to show ethnic differences between Asian and Caucasian subjects on antipsychotics, antidepressants, antianxiety medications, and lithium (Chien, 1989). There may be differences as well where pharmacokinetics (that is, drug metabolism and volume of drug distribution) are concerned. Genetics, diet, and exposure to chemicals may be possible factors in such differences. There may also be pharmacodynamic differences in terms of receptor responsivity of the brain—for instance, among schizophrenics (Lin and Poland, 1989). Indeed, there are more reports that show ethnic differences than those that do not (Chien, 1989).

At this point, however, the findings are not yet conclusive, and newer research techniques (such as computerized electroencephalography) are being considered to directly assess them. Nor has there been any systematic study of psychotropic ethnic differences among Filipino American patients per se. Moreover, psychodynamic and cultural factors are present in every clinical situation and directly affect the use and effectiveness of any medication.

> Vignette. *A sixty-five-year-old Filipino joined his wife in the United States twelve years before consultation. His children were all established and married in their new country, living three hours away.*
>
> *For six months, he had been taking reserpine, an antihypertensive that can cause depression. He was also reacting to the impending loss of his landholdings in the Philippines, due to new governmental decrees. The property meant a lot to him, and the psychodynamic meanings were varied.*

> *Depressed, with weight loss, insomnia and agitation, he initially refused to see a psychiatrist and sought out his internist instead. The psychiatrist, on consultation, advised a change in the antihypertensive and made himself available for treatment of any side effects. The patient had to be "checked" daily and his side effects closely listened to. Through all this, he was able to talk about his impending losses, as well as about feeling loss of control in his new country. His endogenous symptoms responded to 50 mg. of nortriptyline, which he took for one year.*

Electroconvulsive Therapy (ECT)

ECT ("shock treatment") has always been used in the Philippines for the treatment of severe depression and severely agitated psychosis, especially in public mental health settings. ECT is well recognized as an effective form of treatment and well received when prescribed by a respected doctor. The stigma associated with ECT is observably less with first-generation immigrants than with later generations of Filipino Americans.

Cognitive Therapy and Counseling

Directive, concrete instructions are generally well received when given by a respected authority figure. In her study of counseling intervention techniques in a Philippine doctoral program, Salazar-Clemeña (1991) notes that the three most common intervention techniques were the behavioral approach, the active-directive approach, and the cognitive approach. This finding is also in line with her findings on clients' expectations: that the majority of her respondents indicated the need for material help as well as for direct advice. She says that, because of the varied experiences of Filipinos "and the diverse elements of their world view, it seems that a Filipino counseling philosophy must necessarily reflect this diversity. . . . The stress given to feelings as well as cognition and to the material as well as the spiritual implies that Filipinos can be comfortable with a counseling approach that takes all of these into account" (Salazar-Clemeña, 1991, pp. 32–33).

Practical Counseling

Because of the multiple stressors of immigration, patients and their families may call on the therapist for help in many practical aspects of their lives. There may be a need for vocational counseling or for referrals to a neighborhood medical center, the Social Security office, the senior citizens' center, or the local Filipino American social club, and even for directions on using public transportation. In many cases, these aspects are necessary parts of treatment, especially in the adjustment disorders and in the early stage of immigration. Patients negotiating unfamiliar systems in their adopted country may need the therapist to act as a liaison, an advocate, or a case manager.

Indigenous Treatments

Herbs, liniments, prayers, indigenous healers, saints, and local priests are all resorted to, usually by unacculturated Filipino American patients. The therapist should explore the patient's use of these treatment sources because the patient may be embarrassed to share his or her belief in these treatment modalities. Religion is an especially helpful source of strength to a practicing Catholic. The therapist may summon the local priest to the inpatient ward to hear confessions or give Holy Communion to those patients who request them as aids in relieving guilt or hopelessness. Nevertheless, the therapist should also be ready to discern the patient's delusional attitude toward religion and intervene accordingly. According to the patient's depth of religious belief and psychopathology, indigenous healing practices can be used successfully in conjunction with psychotherapy (Kim, 1992; Sustento-Seneriches, 1984).

Conclusion

This chapter has attempted to incorporate psychosociocultural factors to the standard biological methods in treating mentally ill Filipino Americans, with the treatment of depression as the prototype. There is still very meager information on ethnopsychopharmacology for Asians and other ethnic groups. Creative approaches and sensitivity to the unique experiences of the individual—as well as his or her particular ethnic and social background—are important tools in providing mental health services to all ethnic groups.

References

Agoncillo, T. A., and Guerrero, M. C. *History of the Filipino People* (7th ed.). Quezon City, Philippines: Garcia Publishing Company, 1987.

American Psychiatric Association. *Diagnostic and Statistical Manual of Mental Disorders* (3rd ed.). Washington, D.C.: American Psychiatric Association, 1987.

Anderson, J. N. "Health and Illness in Filipino Immigrants." *Western Journal of Medicine,* 1983, *139,* 818–819.

Andres, T. D. *Understanding the Filipino.* Quezon City, Philippines: New Day Publishers, 1987.

Araneta, E. G., Jr. "Filipino Americans." In A. Gaw (ed.), *Cross-Cultural Psychiatry.* Boston: John Wright, 1982.

Araneta, E. G., Jr. "Psychiatric Care of Filipino Americans." In A. Gaw (ed.), *Culture, Ethnicity, and Mental Illness.* Washington, D.C.: American Psychiatric Association, 1993.

Arkoff, A., Thaver, F., and Elkind, L. "Mental Health Counseling Ideas of Asian and American Students." *Journal of Counseling Psychology,* 1966, *13,* 219–223.

Beck, A. T. *Depression: Clinical, Experimental, and Theoretical Aspects.* New York: Holbs, 1967.

Beck, A. T., and others. "An Inventory for Measuring Depression." *Archives of General Psychiatry,* 1961, *4,* 561–571.

Beiser, M. "Influences of Time, Ethnicity, and Attachment on Depression in Southeast Asian Refugees." *American Journal of Psychiatry,* 1988, *145,* 46–51.

Billings, A. G., and Moos, R. H. "Psychosocial Theory and Research in Depression: An Integrative Framework and Review." *Clinical Psychology Review,* 1982, *2,* 213–237.

Bourne, P. "Suicide Among the Chinese in San Francisco." *American Journal of Public Health,* 1973, *63*(8), 744–750.

Bouvier, L. F., and Agresta, A. "The Future of Asian Populations of the United States." In J. T. Fawcett and B. V. Carino (eds.), *Pacific Bridges: The New Immigration from Asia and the Pacific Islands.* Staten Island, N.Y.: Center for Migration Studies, 1987.

Bouvier, L. F., and Martin, P. *Population Change and California's Future.* Washington, D.C.: Population Reference Bureau, 1985.

Brown, T. R., and others. "Mental Illness and the Role of Mental Health Facilities in Chinatown." In W. Sue and N. Wagner (eds.), *Asian Americans: Psychological Perspectives.* Palo Alto, Calif.: Science and Behavior Books, 1973.

Bulatao, J. "Personal Preferences of Filipino Students." Paper presented to the Psychological Association of the Philippines, Manila, 1963.

Bulatao, J. "Hiya." *Philippine Studies,* 1964, *12,* 424–438.

Cabezas, Y. *In Pursuit of Wellness.* San Francisco: California Department of Mental Health, 1982.

Carlota, S. T., and Carlota, A. J. *Legal and Psychological Perspectives on Philippine Juvenile Delinquency.* Quezon City: Law Center, University of the Philippines, 1983.

Catubig, A. "The Filipinos in the Educational System." Paper presented at the second annual conference of the American Association for Filipino Psychology, Berkeley, Calif., 1992.

Cheung, F. M., Law, B. W., and Waldman, E. "Somatization Among Chinese Depressives in General Practice." *International Journal of Psychiatry in Medicine,* 1980–81, *10*(4), 361–373.

Chien, C. "Culture, Ethnicity, and Psychopharmacology." Paper presented at the annual meeting of the American Psychiatric Association, San Francisco, May 1989.

Dean, A., and Lin, N. "The Stress-Buffering Role of Social Support." *Journal of Nervous and Mental Disease,* 1977, *165,* 403–417.

Del Rosario, A. "Child Abuse in the Filipino Community." Unpublished paper, 1990.

Derogatis, L. R., Lipunan, R. S., and Covi, L. "An Outpatient Psychiatric Rating Scale: Preliminary Report." *Psychopharmacology Bulletin,* 1973, *99,* 13–28.

Engel, G. L. "The Need for a New Medical Model: A Challenge for Biomedicine." *Science,* 1977, *196,* 129–136.

Enright, J., and Jaeckle, W. "Psychiatric Symptoms and Diagnosis in Two Subcultures." *International Journal of Social Psychiatry,* 1963, *9,* 12–14.

Enriquez, V. G. *Hellside in Paradise: The Honolulu Youth Gangs.* Report submitted to the Community Affairs Committee, Center for Philippine Studies. Honolulu: University of Hawaii, 1990.

Fawcett, J., Arnold, F., and Minocha, U. "Asian Immigrants to the United States: Flow and Processes." Paper presented at the East-West Population Institute Conference on Asian-Pacific Immigration to the United States, Honolulu, Sept. 1984.

Flaskerud, J., and Soldevilla, E. "Filipino and Vietnamese Clients: Utilizing an Asian Mental Health Center." *Journal of Psychosocial Nursing and Mental Health,* 1986, *24,* 32–36.

Frank, R. G., Kamlet, M. S., and Stoudemire, A. "The Social Cost of Depression." Paper presented at the annual meeting of the American Psychiatric Association, Dallas, May 1985.

Fujii, J. S., Fukushima, S. N., and Yamamoto, J. "Psychiatric Care of Japanese Americans." In A. Gaw (ed.), *Culture, Ethnicity, and Mental Illness.* Washington, D.C.: American Psychiatric Institute, 1993.

Gardner, R. W., Robey, B., and Smith, P. C. *Asian Americans: Growth, Change, and Diversity.* Washington, D.C.: Population Reference Bureau, 1989.

Gaw, A. "Psychiatric Care of Chinese Americans." In A. Gaw (ed.), *Culture, Ethnicity, and Mental Illness.* Washington, D.C.: American Psychiatric Association, 1993.

Gold, M. *The Good News About Depression.* New York: Bantam Books, 1986.

Hamilton, M. "A Rating Scale for Depression." *Journal of Neurology, Neurosurgery and Psychiatry,* 1960, *23,* 56–62.

Hart, D. V. "Filipino Americans: An Emerging Minority." *Amerasia,* 1979, *6,* 173–182.

Ignacio, T. "Tagalog Versus Pilipino Versus Filipino." Paper presented at the conference of the C. E. Smith Museum of Anthropology and the Center for Philippine Studies, California State University, Hayward, 1991.

Jocano, F. L. *Questions and Challenges in Philippine Pre-History.* Quezon City: University of the Philippines Press, 1975.

Jocano, F. L. "Management and Culture: A Normative Approach." Paper presented at the Personnel Management Association of the Philippines Convention, Baguio City, 1981.

Katz, A. "Hospitalization and the Mental Health Service System." In H. I. Kaplan and B. J. Sadock (eds.), *Comprehensive Textbook of Psychiatry.* Baltimore, Md.: Williams and Wilkins, 1989.

Kessler, R. A. "A Strategy for Studying Differential Vulnerability to the Psychological Consequences of Stress." *Journal of Health and Social Behavior,* 1979, *20,* 100–108.

Kim, K. I. "Culture and Mental Illness in Korea." In I. Alissa (ed.), *Handbook of Culture and Mental Illness.* Vol. 5: An International Perspective. New York: Springer-Verlag, 1991.

Kleinman, A. M. "Neurasthenia and Depression: A Study of Somatization and Culture in China." *Cultural and Medical Psychiatry,* 1982, *2,* 2–13.

Kuo, W. H. "Prevalence of Depression Among Asian Americans." *Journal of Nervous and Mental Disease,* 1984, *172,* 449–457.

Ladrido-Ignacio, L., and others. *The Acute Psychosis.* Unpublished report of research findings, National Center of Mental Health, Mandaluyong, Metro Manila, 1985.

Ladrido-Ignacio, L., and Tronco, A. *Primary Health Works.* Manual on mental health prepared for the World Health Organization's Regional Office for the Western Pacific. Manila, Philippines: World Health Organization, 1991.

Lahen, J. *Legal Issues and Guidelines for Nurses Who Care for the Mentally Ill.* Princeton, N.J.: Stack, 1984.

Lamzon, T. *Handbook of Philippine Language Groups.* Quezon City: Manila University Press, 1978.

Lapuz, L. *A Study of Psychopathology.* Quezon City, Philippines: New Day Publishers, 1978.

Lasker, B. *Filipino Immigration to Hawaii and the Continental United States.* New York: Arno Press, 1974.

Lee, H. Y., Hwang, I. K., and Yiu, A. T. "Treatment Methods Before Psychiatric Admission." *Neuropsychiatry,* 1973, *12,* 59–69.

Leong, F. "Counseling and Psychotherapy with Asian Americans: Review of the Literature." *Journal of Counseling Psychology,* 1986, *32*(2), 196–206.

Lieban, R. W. "Traditional Medical Beliefs and the Choice of Practitioners in a Philippine City." *Social Science and Medicine,* 1976, *10,* 289.

Liem, R., and Liem, J. "Social Class and Mental Illness Reconsidered: The Role of Economic Stress and Social Support." *Journal of Health and Social Behavior,* 1978, *19,* 139–156.

Lin, K. M., and Poland, R. "Pharmacotherapy of Asian Psychiatric Patients." *Psychiatric Annals,* 1989, *19*(12), 659–663.

Lott, J. "The Migration of a Mentality: The Pilipino Community." *Social Case Work,* 1976, *57,* 165–172.

Manio, E. "Filipino Values in the Workplace." Paper presented to the Filipino Mental Health Resource Group, San Francisco, Oct. 1990.

Marsella, A. "Depressive Experience and Disorder Across Cultures." In A. C. Triandis and J. G. Dragus (eds.), *Handbook of Cross-Cultural Psychology and Psychopathology.* Boston: Allyn & Bacon, 1980.

Marsella, A., Escudero, M., and Gordon, P. "Stress, Resources, and Symptom Patterns in Urban Filipino Men from Different Age Groups and Social Classes." In W. P. Lebra (ed.), *Transcultural Research in Mental Health.* Honolulu: East–West Coast Center Press, 1972.

Melendy, H. B. "Filipinos in the United States." *Pacific History Review,* 1974, *43,* 521–567.

Moffic, H. S., and Paykel, E. S. "Depression in Medical Inpatients." *Psychiatry,* 1975, *126,* 346–353.

Muñoz, F. M. "Depression-Prevention Research: Conceptual and Practical Considerations." In R. F. Muñoz (ed.), *Depression Prevention.* Washington, D.C.: Hemisphere Publishing Company, 1987.

Muñoz, R. F. "Prevention and Intervention Research: Unipolar Depression." Unpublished paper, 1988.

Murphy, A.B.M. "History of Some Psychiatric Disorders in Southeast Asia." *Philippine Journal of Science,* 1951, *5,* 335.

Nielsen, A. C., and Williams, T. A. "Depression in Ambulatory Medical Patients: Prevalence by Self-Report Questionnaire and Recognition by Nonpsychiatric Physicians." *Archives of General Psychiatry,* 1980, *37,* 999–1004.

Paykel, E. S. "Recent Life Events and Clinical Depression." In E. K. Gunderson and R. H. Rake (eds.), *Life Stress and Illness.* Springfield, Ill.: Thomas, 1974.

Pearlin, L. I., and Schooler, C. "The Structure of Coping." *Journal of Health and Social Behavior,* 1978, *19,* 2–21.

Perlas, A., and Buenaseda, B. "Evaluation of Mental Health Programs." Paper presented at the fourth World Health Organization Coordinating Group Meeting on Mental Health, Manila, Philippines, Feb.–March 1991.

Radloff, L. S. "The CES-D Scale: A Self-Report Depression Scale for Research in the General Population." *Applied Psychological Measurement,* 1977, *1*(3), 385–401.

Rhi, B. Y. "A Preliminary Study of Acculturation Problems in Korea." *Neuropsychiatry,* 1973, *12,* 97–109.

Rhi, B. Y. "Community Mental Health in Korean Culture." Paper presented at the International Symposium on Community Mental Health, Seoul, Korea, July 1989.

Salazar-Clemeña, R. M. *Counseling Psychology in the Philippines: Research and Practice.* Manila, Philippines: De la Salle University Press, 1991.

Sechrest, L. "Culture, Stress, and Psychopathology." In W. Cardill and T. Lin (eds.), *Mental Health Research in Asia and the Pacific.* Honolulu: E. W. Center Press, 1969.

Seligman, M. P. *Helplessness: On Depression, Development, and Death.* San Francisco: Freeman, 1975.

Shon, S. P. *The Filipino Community: A Study of Filipino Americans in Mental Health District 5 of San Francisco.* San Francisco: Mental Health Training Program, Langley Porter Neuropsychiatric Institute, 1977.

Spitzer, R. L., Williams, J. B., and Gibbon, W. *Structured Clinical Interview for DSM-III-R, Patient Version (SCID-P).* New

York: Biometrics Research Department, New York State Psychiatric Institute, 1987.

Sue, S., and McKinney, H. "Asian Americans in the Community Mental Health Care System." *American Journal of Orthopsychiatry,* 1975, *45,* 111–118.

Sue, S., and Morishima, J. K. *The Mental Health of Asian Americans.* San Francisco: Jossey-Bass, 1982.

Sue, S., and Sue, D. W. "MMPI Comparisons Between Asian American and Non-Asian Students Utilizing a Student Health Psychiatric Clinic." *Journal of Counseling Psychology,* 1974, *21,* 423–427.

Sustento-Seneriches, J. "Psychiatric Practice: U.S.A. and the Philippines." Paper presented at the World Psychiatric Association Regional Conference, New York, Oct. 1981.

Sustento-Seneriches, J. "The Traditional Healers and Psychiatry in the Philippine Setting." *Philippine Journal of Psychiatry,* 1984, 11–35.

Sustento-Seneriches, J. "The Family *Bantay* in General Psychiatric Care." Paper presented at the Third Pacific Congress of Psychiatry, Seoul, Korea, 1984.

Sustento-Seneriches, J. "Cultural Issues in Forensic Psychiatry." Paper presented at the conference of the C. E. Smith Museum of Anthropology and the Center for Philippine Studies, California State University, Hayward, 1991.

Sustento-Seneriches, J. "Comparison of Diagnoses Among Filipino Patients Seen in Private Practice, Philippines and the U.S." Paper presented at the Fifth Pacific Rim College of Psychiatrists Meeting, Los Angeles,, 1991.

Sustento-Seneriches, J., and Ladrido-Ignacio, L. *Practical Psychiatry in the Philippine Setting.* Iloilo, Philippines, 1983.

Tan, M. *Usug, Kulam, Pasma: Traditional Concepts of Health and Illness in the Philippines.* Quezon City, Philippines: Alay Kapwa Kilusang Pangkalusugan, 1987.

Teuting, P., Koslow, S. H., and Hirschfeld, R.M.A. *Special Report on Depression Research.* DHHS publication no. ADM 1085. Washington, D.C.: U.S. Department of Health and Human Services, 1981.

Tolentino, E. "Cultural Considerations in the Psychotherapy of Depressed Filipino Patients." Paper presented at the annual meeting of the American Psychiatric Association, New York, May 1990.

Tompar-Tiu, A. "Clinical Depression Among Filipino Americans." Paper presented at the annual meeting of the American Psychiatric Association, New York, May 1990.

Urban Associates. *A Study of Selected Socioeconomic Characteristics of Ethnic Minorities, Based on the 1979 Census.* Vol. 2. Arlington, Va.: Urban Associates, 1974.

U.S. Bureau of the Census. *Asian and Pacific Islander Population in the United States: 1980.* Vol. 2: *Subject Reports.* Washington, D.C.: U.S. Government Printing Office, 1988.

U.S. Bureau of the Census. *Statistical Abstract of the United States: 1991* (111th ed.). Washington, D.C.: U.S. Government Printing Office, 1991.

Vallangca, R. B. *Pinoy: The First Wave of Filipino American History.* San Francisco: Strawberry Hill Press, 1977.

Walker, C. E., and Bonner, G. *The Physically and Sexually Abused Child.* New York: Pergamon Press, 1988.

Weissman, M. M., and Myers, J. K. "Affective Disorders in a U.S. Urban Community: The Use of Research Diagnostic Criteria in an Epidemiological Survey." *Archives of General Psychiatry,* 1978, *35,* 1304–1311.

Westermeyer, J. "Cross-Cultural Psychiatric Assessment." In A. Gaw (ed.), *Culture, Ethnicity, and Mental Illness.* Washington, D.C.: American Psychiatric Association Press, 1993.

Yamamoto, J. "Japanese American Suicides in Los Angeles." In J. Westermeyer and I. Carey (eds.), *Anthropology and Mental Health.* Hawthorne, N.Y.: Mouton, 1976.

Yap, P. M. "Mental Disease Peculiar to Certain Cultures: Survey of Comparative Psychiatry." *Journal of Mental Science,* 1951, *97,* 313.

Zaguirre, J. "Amok." *Journal of the Philippine Federation of Private Medical Practitioners,* 1957, *6*(8).

Zhang, M. "Mental Health Services in Shanghai." Paper presented at the annual meeting of the American Psychiatric Association, New Orleans, May 1991.

Index

E

F

G

H

I